FROM THE HOLY LAND TO GRACELAND

Sacred People, Places and Things in Our Lives

FIG. 1. FANS' MEMORIAL WALL, 1989. PHOTO BY GARY VIKAN. UNLESS OTHERWISE INDICATED, ALL PHOTOS ARE BY THE AUTHOR.

From The Holy Land to Graceland: Sacred People, Places, and Things in Our Lives

Copyright 2012 Gary Vikan. All rights reserved.

Published by The AAM Press of the American Alliance of Museums, 1575 Eye St. NW, Suite 400, Washington, DC 20005
www.aam-us.org

John Strand, Publisher
jstrand@aam-us.org

Susan v. Levine, Designer

ISBN 978-1-933253-72-5

Vikan, Gary.
From the Holy Land to Graceland : sacred people, places and things in
our lives / Gary Vikan.
    pages cm
Includes bibliographical references.
ISBN 978-1-933253-72-5
1. Sacred space--Social aspects. 2. Religious articles--Social
aspects. 3. Historic sites--Religious aspects. 4. Celebrities--Homes
and haunts. 5. Saints--Homes and haunts. 6. Martyrs--Homes and haunts.
7. Religion and culture. 8. Pilgrims and pilgrimages--Social aspects.
9. Presley, Elvis, 1935-1977--Influence. 10. Graceland Mansion
(Memphis, Tenn.) I. Title.
BL580.V55 2012
203'.5--dc23
                        2012035403

FROM THE HOLY LAND TO GRACELAND

Sacred People, Places and Things in Our Lives

Gary Vikan

The AAM Press

TABLE OF CONTENTS

INTRODUCTION

On the night of August 15, 2009, I was among the thousands gathered on Elvis Presley Boulevard in the sticky Memphis heat. I had been in that same spot on that same date in 1989. Surprisingly little had changed in 20 years—except, of course, for the emergence of a new generation of ardent Presley fans. The Candlelight Vigil, the dramatic culmination of Elvis Week, was and still remains an extraordinary phenomenon, though only the most prominent among many phenomena that make Elvis, Graceland, Elvis Week, and Presley pilgrims a compelling puzzle.

FIG. 2.

More than 1,700 books have been written about some aspect of Elvis Presley. Most cover familiar territory in a familiar way. Many have some insider authorship, including Elvis's former wife, Priscilla, as well as his uncle, cook, housekeeper, nurse, body guard, and so on. *From The Holy Land to Graceland*, however, stands apart among Elvis books insofar as it offers an interpretation of Elvis, Graceland, Elvis Week, and Presley pilgrims through the lens of early Christian saints, holy places, and pilgrimage, and their contemporary counterparts, both Christian (*El Sanctuario de Chimayo*) and secular (Ground Zero). This book draws as well upon the work of social theorists and anthropologists, including Max Weber, for his concept of the secular charismatic, and Edith and Victor Turner, for their analysis of pilgrimage and, more specifically, for their concepts of *communitas* and liminality.

My qualifications for this approach are appropriate to the task. Soon after receiving my Ph.D. in medieval art from Princeton University, I began to focus my research on early Christian pilgrimage and pilgrimage art, saints, relics, and icons at the Harvard Center for Byzantine Studies at Dumbarton Oaks, in Washington, D.C. My 1982 book, *Byzantine Pilgrimage Art,* recently republished in a revised edition, captures and reflects my work and point of view. Along the way, I had the benefit of studying with Harvard sociologist Stanley Tambiah, through whom I became acquainted with Weber and the Turners.

In the end, the intent of this book is to convince the reader that Graceland is much more than a popular tourist destination associated with a famous entertainer, and that Elvis Presley is much more than the King of Rock 'n' Roll. Rather, that the former is a *locus sanctus* ("holy place") and the latter its resident saint—and that the hordes of fans standing in the heat on Elvis Presley Boulevard each August 15 are its pilgrims. Once these roles are identified and acknowledged, an elegant simplicity emerges, which is easily transferable to such emerging secular saints as Michael Jackson and to such emerging holy places as Ground Zero. Moreover, the reader will, along the way, become acquainted with some of the basic building blocks of Christianity, both historically and in our own time, including saints and their "lives" (*vitae*), icons and iconography, holy places and their sacred calendars, relics, souvenirs, and votives. The inevitable conclusion is that the "saints" of our day are our martyred secular charismatics, of which Elvis Presley is, literally, the King.

But the reader should not expect total coincidence of the 21st and the 5th centuries in this regard. Indeed, it is striking that among the inscriptions on the Fans' Memorial Wall at Graceland, in Presley tabloid articles, and in Elvis mythic literature more generally, there is seldom any hint of Elvis as the recipient of prayer, even when he is clearly the proximate source of the miraculous, and even when the context is richly flavored with conventional Christianity. Only occasionally is God or Jesus mentioned and rarely is there any talk of Elvis as being an intercessor. In this respect, Elvis's "sainthood" is strikingly different from the conventional Christian sort, wherein the role of one's spiritual friend as one's advocate before God is always central. Though of course, sainthood, either as performed or as acknowledged, is not a constant, even in Christianity. The great martyrs mostly date from before the Peace of the Church (AD 313) and "standing on a column" as an expression of saintly piety went out of fashion more than a millennium ago. As the early Christian saint was a product of and a window onto that world, Elvis Presley, and those of our day like him, are a product of and a window onto our world. Or, in the words of Elvis fan Anna Norman, on the Fans' Memorial Wall: "Elvis, you've become such an icon for our time."

Given my background, it was probably inevitable that I would have a moment of epiphany on August 12, 1987, when I opened the *Washington Post* and reencountered Elvis Presley by way of an article datelined Graceland, with the startling headline "Saint Elvis." Of course, I understood this Elvis to be one and the same with the gyrating rock 'n' roller I first became acquainted with as a pre-teen in the mid-1950s, by way of Sun Records and my sister's 45 record player. And identical as well with the overweight, bombastic Vegas crooner of the 1970s, whose bizarre physical and mental decline occasionally caught my attention by way of a short paragraph in the daily newspapers about his hospital stays, in rooms made dark 24/7 with aluminum foil, to "clear an obstructed colon." All of that was both familiar and pretty much irrelevant to me as I moved on in my pop music preferences to the Beatles and as I became a serious student of early Christian art and culture. That is, until that *Washington Post* article, exactly ten years to the week after Elvis' death at age 42 on the toilet in his second-floor bathroom at Graceland. The world in and around Graceland that the *Post* reporter described unfolding before his eyes during Elvis International Tribute Week a decade after the fact was immediately familiar to me from my research on early Christian holy sites: pilgrimage, relics, miracles, sacred souvenirs, votives, and, of course, the notion of a resident saint. This was a world I understood, and so I began a sideline of Elvis research, which led to Elvis lectures, then to an article, "Graceland as *Locus Sanctus*," in an exhibition catalogue entitled *Elvis + Marilyn: 2x Immortal*, to Elvis courses at Johns Hopkins University and Goucher College, and finally, to this book—which owes much to the insights of my students over the years.

My Graceland-related research has drawn me not only again to Jerusalem, and multiple times to Memphis, but also to a variety of Christian *loca sancta* in North America and Europe, including the "dirt shrine" of Our Lord of Esquipulas in Chimayo, north of Santa Fe, and the "oil shrine" of Brother André in Montreal, as well as to the "water shrine" of Our Lady of Lourdes, in southwestern France, and to the Shrine of Our Lady of Guadalupe, in Mexico City, with its peasant's cloak bearing a miraculous image of the Virgin Mary. Along the way I have had power-fully affective experiences of objectified charisma—of the localized sacred—honor-ing victims of unjust death, from the 16th Street Baptist Church in Birmingham, Alabama, to Auschwitz-Birkenau near Krakow, in Poland, to Ground Zero in Lower Manhattan. Moreover, I have sought out and explored some of the most famous dead-celebrity *loca sancta*, including that of John F. Kennedy at the Grassy Knoll in Dallas, that of Martin Luther King, Jr. at the Lorraine Motel in Memphis, that of Harvey Milk in the Castro District of San Francisco, that of Marilyn Monroe in Westwood Memorial Park in Los Angeles, and, in Paris, those of Princess Diana at the Place de l'Alma and Jim Morrison in Père-Lachaise Cemetery. Roadside shrines to accident victims have their place in this study as well. And finally, I have more recently added Michael Jackson to my list of the charismatic dead, beginning with my visit to his Star on the Walk of Fame in Hollywood, shortly after his death. The intent of all of this on-site research was to provide a broader and more nuanced con-text historically and in our own lives for situating the Elvis/Graceland phenomenon.

My sources, assembled in the Bibliography at the end of this book, draw on a wide range of academic fields, from the history of religion to medieval art history, to social anthropology, to consumer psychology, to contemporary popular culture. As for primary sources, for the early Christian period I rely heavily on the *vitae* of my favorite holy man, Simeon the Stylite, who lived in northern Syria in the first half of the 5th century, and on the engaging diary of a pilgrim from Piacenza, in northern Italy, who chronicled in rich detail his pilgrimage, around 570, to the famous sites and shrines associated with the life of Christ in the Holy Land. These are complemented in many cases by the surviving ruins of the shrines themselves, as well as by associated pilgrims' artifacts for transporting sacred souvenirs (oil, dirt), and by pilgrim votives left behind.

For Graceland and Elvis there are multiple sources beyond the main one, which is my own on-site observation and photography (most of the photographs reproduced in this book are my own). The standard Elvis biography, in two volumes, is by Peter Guralnick: *Last Train to Memphis* from 1994 and *Careless Love* from 1999. More recently, there is Susan Doll's *Elvis for Dummies*, which is a ready and reliable source for Elvis facts. For a wealth of pictures of all things Elvis, nothing tops Jane and Michael Stern's *Elvis World* from 1987, and for the fan quotes to go with them, Erika Doss's *Elvis Culture: Fans, Faith, and Image* from 1999. Beyond these, I draw on many publications on Elvis directed toward the popular market that are, in effect, modern counterparts to the early Christian saints' *vitae*, insofar as they freely mix fact and fiction, and are thoroughly propagandistic. There are plenty of references to *The New York Times*, but I have included as well a number of citations and pictures from the tabloids, especially the *Weekly World News*, because, like popular Elvis literature, these newspapers provide a widow onto Elvis belief.

FIG. 3

How can we trust a category of print medium that has documented on its front page for May 25, 1993 the discovery in Israel of the skull of Goliath with David's fatal stone still embedded in its forehead? Do these weeklies speak for anyone's truth? Sometimes I wonder, but this much I do know: when the *Weekly World News* was on its binge of Elvis sightings, 20 years ago, there were two TV specials hosted by Bill Bixby called "Is Elvis Alive?" Bixby and others presented the evidence for the "living Elvis" with some earnestness, and as they did, an on-screen tally was being taken of those responding by phone to the question at hand: *is* Elvis alive? The vast majority said yes.

This book falls into three sections that build sequentially on one another. Section I, *Elvis as Saint*, is about the "who," as it explores what it takes to be a saint in Christianity, the notion of charisma and secular charismatics, and the characteristic manifestations of charismatics whether religious or secular, including martyrdom, miracles, relics, *vitae*, icons, and iconography. Section II, *Graceland as Locus Sanctus*, is about the "where," as it examines the saint's home or *locus sanctus*. In order to put Graceland in a broad context, this chapter includes both early and post-medieval Christian holy sites, as well as modern *loca sancta* for victims of unjust death and for political and entertainment charismatic martyrs. The intent is to reveal how holy sites come into existence and what they typically include, in order to position Graceland among them. The final part of the book, Section III, *Graceland Visitors as Pilgrims*, is about the "how" of the Elvis/Graceland phenomenon, as it is revealed by populating the *locus santus* and then exploring why Presley pilgrims go on pilgrimage when they do, what they do on site, what they take away, and what they leave behind.

Why Elvis? Insofar as the Elvis/Graceland mix differs from others like it that I might have chosen to explore instead, it probably differs more in degree than in kind: 50,000 gathered at Graceland for the 10th anniversary of Elvis Presley's death, whereas just a few hundred gathered at the Dakota for the 10th anniversary of John Lennon's death; on any given day 2,000 or more will pass through Graceland's Meditation Garden, whereas just a couple dozen Morrison devotees will find Jim's grave in Père-Lachaise Cemetery—and the same scale differentiation holds true as well for the grave shrine of Bob Marley in the little town of 9 Mile in northern Jamaica and that of Selena, the "Mexican Madonna," in Corpus Christi, Texas.

Or consider Marilyn Monroe, with whom Elvis shared equal billing in the Boston Contemporary's 1994 traveling exhibition *Elvis + Marilyn: X2 Immortal*. There is an intriguing display of celebrity shoes at The Bata Shoe Museum in Toronto. A pair of shiny Elvis loafers is set next to a pair of bright red high heels once belonging to Marilyn Monroe; they, and shoes belonging to a few other famous people, are sequentially highlighted in the darkened display case as film clips capturing characteristic moments in the lives of their respective wearers appear on a screen at the back. From this display one might infer that the respective graves of Elvis and Marilyn might be similarly distinguished and visited, though in fact, a visit to Marilyn's grave in Westwood Memorial Park, Los Angeles, is revealing of a huge postmortem gulf between the two. Marilyn Monroe's vault is distinguished from its neighbors by a single small floral votive and the imprint of a recent lipstick kiss or two; it receives only a few more visitors daily than the nearby vault of Dean Martin or the tombstone of Rodney Dangerfield.

If we use the model for differentiating hurricanes, Elvis/Graceland is certainly a Category 5—which would make Jim Morrison/Père-Lachaise a Category 1, or perhaps just a tropical storm. But certainly, they are fundamentally the same. The analytical model of the Center for Disease Control may be more useful here, since it differentiates among *etiology* or "cause," *phenomenology*, which is the aggregate of symptoms, the "presentation" in the individual, and *epidemiology*, which is the pattern of distribution among the general population, the "demographic intensity." What sets the Elvis/Graceland combination apart is its epidemiology, its sheer scale, and probably also its phenomenology, its intensity as presented in the individual. For an excellent primer in the extremes of the latter, one need only view Tom Corboy's *Mondo Elvis: The Strange Rites & Rituals of the King's Most Devoted Disciples* from 1984, and therein meet Artie "Elvis" Mentz, the EP tribute artist who equates his relationship to the King to that of a priest to God, since both are filling in for "someone not there in body." (Artie continues to pursue his Elvis mission from his home base in Dubuque, Iowa.) The documentary also features Jenny and Judy Carroll, 20-something twins who claim Elvis as their biological father because they look just like him—which they do, down to their "little cut-off lips." The twins admit occasionally to inviting men over, as they claim, "to play Yahtzee" (as opposed to "hopping in the sack"), but their house rules are strict: "...if they don't like our Elvis Presley music then they get thrown out on their ass...and if they say anything against God or Elvis they get thrown out on their ass again." And then there is the overweight young woman standing in front of Melody Gate at Graceland, proudly showing off a snapshot she took during an earlier Elvis pilgrimage, only later to discover that the cloud formation overhead at that very moment in Graceland revealed a profile portrait of the King—which it did. Her conclusion? "Elvis was watching what was going on at Graceland."

Corboy's devoted disciples of the King would certainly rank at the top of the "celebrity worship scale" recently developed in Britain by a group of psychologists. Their lowest, most tepid group of worshipers comprises those who do little more celebrity-wise than keep up with the latest tidbits of gossip trough various fan communication vehicles, whereas worshipers in the next level up add to that currency of knowledge a menu of celebrity-based social interactions with like fans. These are the folks who join the fan clubs. Then at the top, at the most intense level in this scientific scale of celebrity worship, are the truly freakish fans. Repugnant to outsiders but fully understood and embraced by those within their own bizarre devotional circle, these hyper-fans are characterized by an intensely personal, potentially pathological identification with their chosen celebrity. This will typically bring with it a distorted view of the world and of their role in it—a view that will likely jeopardize their careers and families, as well as their emotional and physical health. The most compelling voice in *Mondo Elvis*, a bleach-blonde, middle-aged chain-smoker named Frankie Horrocks, fits this top-of-the-scale profile perfectly. Frankie's intense passion for Elvis, which began with her first viewing of *Blue Hawaii*, propelled her abrupt relocation to Memphis after Elvis' death, her subsequent divorce from her husband (as she says, on the grounds of "excessive devotion to Elvis"), and her estrangement from her son, who didn't want to leave New Jersey. Tragically, Frankie's Elvis-loving daughter, who came with her to Memphis, was murdered by a madman and buried in a dress she once wore to an Elvis concert.

As for etiology, whether we're considering the Holy Land, Graceland or the Grassy Knoll in Dallas—Jesus, Elvis, or John F. Kennedy—the question of the root cause of our propensity to objectify charismatic power in people, places, and things, and to seek its transfer to ourselves through touch and imitative behavior, lies beyond the scope of comparative religion. Rather, it is to be sought in the realm of social anthropology and, at its most basic level, in evolutionary biology and in the patterns of magical thinking that are its modern-day, hardwired residue in our heads. (Magical thinking actually works. A recent study showed that amateur golfers made 38% more of their putts when they used a putter that was said to have belonged to a PGA champion.)

While he could not then have understood their neurological basis, the famous Scottish social anthropologist James George Frazer succinctly defined these inter-related phenomena in 1890. In chapter 3 of *The Golden Bough*, Frazer developed the concept of "sympathetic magic"—a principle by which "things act on each other at a distance through a secret sympathy." And he further divided sympathetic magic into two branches: homeopathic magic (the law of similarity) and contagious magic (the law of contact). Both—the magical thinking underlying imitative behavior or *mimesis* and the magical thinking underlying touch or contagion—will figure promi-nently in this book.

What all this means is that while the idiom of Elvis's charismatic performance might seem to mirror that of a Pentecostal minister, or that the idiom of Graceland pilgrimage might seem to mirror that of an early Christian holy site, it should not imply and certainly does not require causality. On the contrary, such resonances suggest that our susceptibility to the power of charisma and our preoccupation with its objectification in people, places, and things are primal (i.e., neurological), a-his-torical, and cross-cultural. Inevitably, charisma will manifest itself in similar though potentially fully independent ways.

There is the question of whether there will ever be another Graceland: will, for example, the postmortem Michael Jackson, the King of Pop, reach the "cult" level of postmortem Elvis, the King of Rock 'n' Roll? On the first anniversary of Jackson's death, June 25, 2010, a Swarovski crystal-studded glove he wore on his 1984 Victory Tour sold at auction in Las Vegas for $192,000, more than six times the estimate. And that same day, Thriller dances were scheduled for cities across the globe, reprising those that formed spontaneously a year earlier as news of Michael's death spread; there was as well a live cam feed from the Mausoleum at Forrest Lawn Cemetery in Glendale, where Michael's body resides. Whether or not Michael/ Neverland will ever reach the Category 5 level, it is pretty certain that there will never be a dynastic successor in the rock 'n' roll-pop music lineage to which both Presley and Jackson belong. The balkanization of the world's musical tastes along with the demise of the recording industry that supported both superstars ensures that outcome. As does its corollary, namely, the proliferation of a multiplicity of Internet vehicles for connecting a nearly infinite number of niche musical artists with a nearly infinite number of niche fan groups; thus, the intense but relatively small and ethnically circumscribed cohort group that nourishes the memory of Selena, star of Latino Pop. This is a world far different from that of 1956, when Elvis' first appearance on the *Ed Sullivan Show* was seen by 54 million Americans, which was more than 82% of the viewing public. Or from the world of the *Elvis—Aloha from Hawaii* concert of 1973, when more than 90 percent of all Japanese television sets were tuned in. This means that even if someday Neverland joins Graceland as a secular descendent of the Holy Land, they will almost certainly be the last of their type. This does not mean, of course, that there will not be successors to the Grassy Knoll, Ground Zero, and Auschwitz, for there certainly will be.

On a more personal level, the answer to "Why Elvis?" is embedded in the iconography of a photograph that my father took of me at a Cub Scout promotion ceremony in 1957 (fig. 4). The picture was taken in the basement of Hope Lutheran Church, my family's church, in Fosston, Minnesota. This is my hometown, a farming community of about 1,500 folks, mostly of Scandinavian descent, in frozen north-western Minnesota, where, as they say, "The Prairie meets the Pines." My father published the local weekly newspaper and, given his tiny staff, he was both its only reporter and its photographer. His reporting and photo documentation included the annual East Polk County Fair, the occasional house fire and car accident, the extraordinary birth of a two-headed calf—and yes, Cub Scout promotion ceremo-nies that might be staged in any one of our four Lutheran churches. To the extent we had a galvanizing local hero, it was Paul Bunyan and his Blue Ox "Babe," in super-human scale rendered, in 1937, in painted concrete on the shores of Lake Bemidji, 40 miles east of Fosston on Interstate 2. There are two revealing clues to my future and this book in that photograph of 1957: my elaborate Wild-Root-empowered hairdo, which was clearly modeled after that of 1957 Elvis, and the framed picture of Jesus in the background. I happen to be standing in precisely the spot that seems to have Jesus speaking into my right ear. This is Warner Sallman's famous version of Jesus from 1940—the most reproduced of all Jesus pictures in the world, and the one that I grew up with.

At that point in my life, I was simultaneously attuned both to Jesus and to Elvis, as to some degree many of my generation were. For most of us, Elvis was exotic in the extreme, and we loved him for that. Our Hope Lutheran Church Jesus, on the other hand, was not, and by age 13 my own enthusiasm for him and the belief package he represented had all but disappeared. Upstairs in the sanctuary of the church, Jesus appears again, this time in the form of a plaster copy of the famous Danish neoclassical sculptor Bertel Thorvaldsen's *Christus* of 1838—which is the form he took on many American Protestant altars of the period. Life-size, with robes

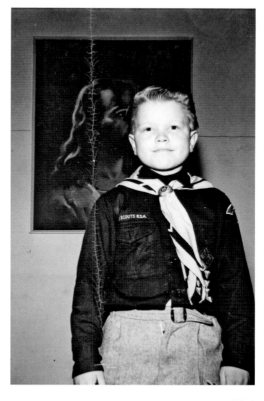

FIG. 4

colored in muted pastel tones, Thorvaldsen's Jesus and the elaborately carved but unpainted wooden altarpiece behind him dominate the interior of the remarkably spare sanctuary of Hope Lutheran Church. This is Jesus as I knew him and this is religion as I knew it: devoid of the blood and gore of the Passion, of sacred bodies and holy bones, and of the exotic saints that could have helped me find what I had lost, or get our family safely home from Sunday dinner at our grandmother's house, 70 miles distant in Grand Forks, North Dakota. I think I must even then have been jealous of those few Catholics in town, with their glowing red altar light, their black-draped nuns, their reliquaries, and their brightly-painted statuary of all sorts of holy people. For me, Elvis supplied everything I thought I was missing, and more.

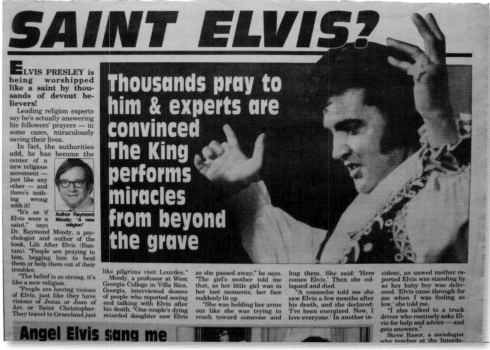

The newspaper clipping text reads:

SAINT ELVIS?

ELVIS PRESLEY is being worshipped like a saint by thousands of devout believers!

Leading religion experts say he's actually answering his followers' prayers — in some cases, miraculously saving their lives.

In fact, the authorities add, he has become the center of a new religious movement — just like any other — and there's nothing wrong with it!

"It's as if Elvis were a saint," says Dr. Raymond Moody, a psychologist and author of the book, Life After Elvis (Bantam). "People are praying to him, begging him to heal them or help them out of their troubles.

"The belief is so strong, it's like a new religion.

"People are having visions of Elvis, just like they have visions of Jesus or Joan of Arc or Saint Christopher. They travel to Graceland just

Author Raymond Moody: "A new religion"

Thousands pray to him & experts are convinced The King performs miracles from beyond the grave

like pilgrims visit Lourdes."

Moody, a professor at West Georgia College in Villa Rica, Georgia, interviewed dozens of people who reported seeing and talking with Elvis after his death. "One couple's dying retarded daughter saw Elvis

as she passed away," he says. "The girl's mother told me that, as her little girl was in her last moments, her face suddenly lit up.

"She was holding her arms out like she was trying to reach toward someone and

hug them. She said: 'Here comes Elvis.' Then she collapsed and died.

"A counselor told me she saw Elvis a few months after his death, and she declared: 'I've been energized. Now, I love everyone.' In another in-

cident, an unwed mother reported Elvis was standing by as her baby boy was delivered. 'Elvis came through for me when I was feeling so low,' she told me.

"I also talked to a truck driver who routinely asks Elvis for help and advice — and gets answers."

Steve Rasor, a sociologist who teaches at the Interde-

Angel Elvis sang me

FIG. 5

I.
ELVIS *as* SAINT

The notion that Elvis Presley is an extraordinary religious figure, possibly even a saint, has been proclaimed not only by *The Washington Post* but also, as one would expect, by the tabloids (fig. 5). The idea has been current since the '80s, receiving re-endorsement on Elvis's 75th birthday in an article in the *Post*'s "Under God" section, wherein David Waters ruminates on the relationship between Elvis and Jesus, and tallies his reputed multiple baptisms into some very potent "spiritual mojo." But Waters, like all of the other advocates for some kind of Elvis sainthood, begs the question of what it takes to become a saint in the first place. As charismatic mediating agents between our everyday world and remote and powerful spiritual forces, saints ("holy people") have existed in all religions and outside conventional religion as well. The context of sainthood for

Elvis Presley, given his religious background and the background of his fan base, is clearly understood to be Christian. But of what sort?

Were it a question for Elvis of official canonization by the Roman Catholic Church, the notion of Saint Elvis would be met with ridicule, not for lack of possible Elvis miracles, but rather for Elvis'ss obvious failure to live an exemplary, virtuous, and specifically Catholic life—and in so doing, demonstrating what the Vatican calls the "heroic virtues." And in any event, the complex bureaucratic path leading to the lofty designation of saint in Catholicism, which ultimately leads to the desk of the Pope himself, is one that only the rarest of virtuous Catholic miracle-worker heroes nowadays successfully ascends. A review of the six necessary steps laid out in the Apostolic Constitution *Divinus Perfectionis Magister,* promulgated in 1983 by John Paul II, is daunting indeed, and goes a long way toward explaining why there have been only five successful nominations for sainthood in the history of Catholicism in America.

The most recent nomination and still a work in progress involves a 19th-century Maryland priest from Germany named Francis X. Seelos, the Divine Physician; a tiny sliver of his breastbone and his intercession are believed by an elderly Annapolis woman to have miraculously rid her of a multitude of cancers and saved her from near-term death. By all accounts, Father Seelos, the "cheerful ascetic," had led an exemplary Catholic life, up until his death in 1867 at age 48 from Yellow Fever, as he attended to plague victims in New Orleans. Thanks to a documented healing in the Baltimore Archdiocese in the early 1970s (this time involving liver cancer), Father Seelos was Beatified at a ceremony in the Vatican in 2000. After that, a committee was appointed by the local Archdiocese to take depositions from 11 witnesses, including doctors, nurses, friends, and, of course, the patient herself, in order to document a second miracle, and thus to enable the final and most difficult step upward to sainthood. Once assembled, this evidence will be sent on to the Vatican to be reviewed and reviewed yet again, in a slow-motion vetting process that usually lasts for decades, and can grind to a halt if advocacy wanes. John Paul's promulgation of 1983 speeded the process somewhat by removing the office of the Promoter General of the Faith, which played the role of the devil's advocate, raising and probing any objections to or doubts about moving forward toward sainthood.

The effect of this streamlining is likely to be realized first in John Paul's own accelerated ascent to sainthood.

Canonization by the Catholic Church is just one of several paths to Christian sainthood, and by far the most difficult one, at that. Actually, the *de jure* form of saint-making as now practiced by the Vatican was only a development of the second millennium, and the Orthodox Church still follows a practice closer to the *de facto* saint-making common among the early Christians. About a third of the 264 dead popes are saints, but the vast majority of these were elected by popular acclaim in the first millennium, and many were martyrs; only five were canonized in the second millennium. Pope John Paul II's enormous popularity carried with it the potential to set Catholic practice back one thousand years: not only did shouts of "Santo subito!" erupt during his funeral mass, John Paul's successor, Pope Benedict XVI, presided over his beatification on May 1, 2011, after having waved the traditional five-year wait and beginning the beatification process just weeks after his predecessor's death. By the old-fashioned loose rules of popular acclamation, someone is informally elected to sainthood by the collective belief and actions of his followers. A wide variety of lifestyles is tolerated among potential candidates for this popular form of canonization, and while some evidence of miracle-working is usually expected and incorruptibility of the flesh (a body that does not decay) is more than useful, in the end, an unjust death may be enough to earn the victim the title of saint.

Father John Karastamatis, a Greek Orthodox priest serving in the Santa Cruz, California, parish of St. Elias was brutally murdered by "Satanists" inside his church on the night of May 18, 1985. The Saint Herman of Alaska Brotherhood in Anchorage, where Father John had once served, soon took the initiative to elevate him to the status of martyr saint, declaring as unnecessary "some 'official' ecclesiastical statement" in favor of the tradition that saints are created "according to the testimony of the faithful, by 'popular demand'." But even though there is a miracle attributed to Father John—the church bells on his native Greek island of Andros spontaneously rang out at the arrival there of a piece of his clothing—there has not been a ground swell on his behalf, and the Orthodox Church hierarchy has yet to offer its endorsement. Should that eventually come, the Church would, as it has for centuries, then help promulgate an accepted image (icon) of Saint John of Santa Cruz as well as an official *vita*.

Heidi Bradner for The New York Times

FIG. 6

Or consider the more recent story of Evgeniy Rodionov, Soldier Martyr of the Russian Orthodox Church (fig. 6). Evgeniy was beheaded on May 23, 1996, on his 19th birthday, by a Chechnyan field commander who claimed he killed Rodionov after he refused to convert to Islam and to give up his Orthodox crucifix. His mother Lyubov eventually ransomed her son's headless body and, with the help of church officials, returned it to their village west of Moscow and re-buried it on a hillside next to a simple whitewashed church. Despite the growing discomfort of the official Russian Orthodox Church, Evgeniy Rodionov's grave is becoming a pilgrimage destination, especially for soldiers, some of whom leave their war medals as votives. Icons of "Zhenya," as he is affectionately called, are now commonplace in Russia; a full-length image of him in his camouflage uniform, with rifle, hat, and halo, is paired with a traditional icon of the Virgin and Child at the altar in a church near St. Petersburg. Unofficial prayer cards of Soldier Martyr Rodionov are in wide circulation, with a picture of the saint on one side and, on the other side, words crediting Yevgeny with having "brought down his torturers" and defeating "the powerless insolence of demons," and concluding with "through his prayers save our souls." As for miracles, believers say that his icons sometimes give forth drops of sacred perfume; Evgeniy's mother takes care to plan her travels through the guidance of these sacred emissions.

There's no question: Elvis did not live an exemplary Christian life. But during the course of this centuries-long practice of popular saint-making, Christianity has welcomed saints of vastly varying backgrounds, including those unrecognized by their contemporaries. The Russians have long had an interesting category of saint called the *Yurodivy* or "Holy Fools," whose spiritual mission in life was to live outside the norms of society, pretty much as street people, imitating Christ by rejecting worldly cares and enduring humiliation. Often loopy and sometimes naked, Holy Fools were ignored or perhaps even abused in their lifetimes but acknowledged and venerated after death.

The uncorrupted body of a recent entry in the revered lineage of *Yurodivy* can be found in San Francisco. Saint John Maximovich of Shanghai and San Francisco (1896-1966) lies in full ecclesiastic garb in his elaborate shrine at the right of the sanctuary of the grand Russian-style Cathedral of the Mother of God, Joy of All Who Sorrow, on Geary Street. John, a native of Ukraine who made his way to San Francisco by way of Belgrade, Shanghai, and Paris, was canonized in July 1994 by the Russian Orthodox Church Outside of Russia (ROCOR). He earned this posthumous honor in part because of that intact (though now dark brown and thoroughly desiccated) corpse of his, in part because of the miracles he performed (notably, predicting the date of his own death), in part because of his extraordinary spiritual exertions, which included sleeping exclusively in a (still-surviving and now venerate) chair and only for a few hours each night for more than 40 years, and in part because of his Holy-Fool-like ways. The latter included John's simple speech and manner, and the fact that he would take his shoes off and give them away, thus walking barefoot, even on the coldest days. Saint-making traditions endure and yet they are adaptable to evolving technology; Saint John can now be venerated from the comfort of your home or office, via his Facebook page.

And then, of course, there is the ever-popular but thoroughly mythical Saint Christopher, whose feast day was officially withdrawn from the Roman Catholic calendar of saints in 1969. Despite this demotion, Christopher continues to provide safe transport for his theologically uninformed followers from the dashboards of cars and trucks all over the world. On the back of his prayer card is the plea to the non-saint to "make me feel this car," and to "serve mankind [and not] destroy."

FIG. 7

The lives of some of Christianity's most famous holy men were bizarre in the extreme, making Elvis's sometimes odd behavior seem almost normal by comparison. Certainly, one of Christianity's strangest holy men was a stylite ("column dweller") named Simeon, who lived in the first half of the 5th century (fig. 7). Saint Simeon earned the title of stylite because he spent nearly four decades in fasting, prayer, and miracle-working atop a series of ever-taller columns rising above a barren patch of what is now northern Syria, near the town of Aleppo. What set Simeon apart from nearly everyone who aspired to saintliness at that time was not only his column-dwelling, but also the way he gave expression to his beliefs through a life-long commitment to ever-increasing bodily austerities, especially fasting and the mortification of his flesh. For these exertions, Simeon earned the saintly title of ascetic ("one who labors").

Born into a poor shepherd's family, Simeon developed an intense devotion to Christianity in early adolescence, apparently after he and his brother stumbled into a church, and he, in particular, was taken with its smell of the incense styrax. Simeon left home as a teenager without telling his parents, and entered a nearby monastery. But before long, he was expelled because of his extreme behavior: not only did Simeon refuse to eat during the entire 40 days of Lent, he secretly bound his waist so tightly with a palm-frond rope that it took three days of soaking to pull the fibers from his wounds. (The smell of his putrid flesh had eventually attracted the attention of the brothers.) After that, Simeon shut himself up in a hut for more than a year, again refusing both food and water during all of Lent; moreover, he took to standing upright for days, as long as his limbs would sustain him. For a time, he lived on a hillside in an enclosure he laid out with stones; a chain shackled to his foot was affixed to a rock at the center of the enclosure. The word was rapidly spreading that Simeon's survival in the face of all this fasting and self punishment was itself a miracle. Crowds of pilgrims arrived seeking his counsel and prayers, and eventually, this left Simeon too little time for his own devotions.

At the age of about 30, Simeon sought vertical escape from his followers by mounting a column he had discovered in some abandoned ruins; it was less than ten feet tall. Over the next 37 years, Simeon graduated to ever taller columns, topping out at more than 50 feet. Lent was his time of extreme austerity, which even as he passed into middle age meant no food or water; this required that he eventually sit and then lie down because of his self-imposed weakness. He joyfully nourished maggots in the open wounds he developed under his hair shirt, acknowledged with a saint's pride his chronic constipation, and every day bowed his head to his feet in prayer more than 1000 times; one amazed visitor gave up counting at 1,244 genuflections. When he was not bowing, Simeon prayed with head erect and arms stretched out horizontally in imitation of the crucifixion of Christ. Yet all the while, Simeon the Stylite remained accessible to the thousands of worshippers who gathered around his column, in need of healing, comfort, or advice. These included, over the years, at least three emperors, one of whom communicated with the saint by letter for advice on troubling theological matters.

When Simeon the Stylite died in the late summer of 459, his body was ceremoniously escorted to Antioch by seven bishops and the military commander of the Byzantine army of the east, together with a contingent of 600 soldiers; following was a throng of unruly pilgrims. The reason for the escort was simple: Simeon's followers wanted to divide up his body for relics. A sense from our own time of that procession and the crush of the faithful to get close can be evoked via YouTube's capture of the procession of the body of Pope John Paul II from the Apostolic Palace to St. Peter's Basilica on April 4, 2005, two days after his death. But for the absolute chaos and franetic grasping for relics, there is nothing more extreme and disturbing than the arrival of the body of Ayatollah Khomeini by helicopter at the Behesht-e-Zahara Cemetery outside Tehran on June 6, 1989, when the frenzied crowd of more than 2 million jostled the body out of its coffin—again, as captured on YouTube.

Elvis *as* Secular Charismatic Martyr

The stickiness of the word "saint" for Elvis may be avoided entirely by adopting Max Weber's non-religious, value-neutral terminology that centers instead on the word charisma, or "gift." Weber identified the charismatic as possessing qualities that set him apart from ordinary people who, in turn, "endowed" the charismatic with "supernatural, superhuman, or at least specifically exceptional powers or qualities." Significantly, this extraordinary individual is identifiable not by any specific behavioral or physical characteristics, but rather by the impact he has on others, by how he is "treated as endowed" by his followers. This "affectual action" definition (Weber's term) is especially critical for saints whose lifestyles strike non-followers as inappropriate, since what counts is not saint-like behavior but audience reception and reaction. The saint need never in fact have existed, for, like the legendary Saint Christopher, he is created and re-created to suit his evolving base of believers.

Weber's value-neutral approach to charisma shifts emphasis away from the source of the charismatic gift, as a grace from God or as a reward for an exemplary life, to its recognition. This allows for the existence among the ranks of charismatic martyrs of Jesus Malverde, a mustachioed Robin Hood-like brigand who was hanged as a bandit in Culiacan, Mexico, in 1909. Today Malverde is venerated among Mexicans and Mexican-Americans as a saint, with an impressive list of attributed miracles, his own chapel-shrine with votives, including pictures of marijuana plants and AK-47s, and an unmistakable iconic facial type, conjured up in the 1980s by a former street vendor named Eligio González, who believed that he had survived being knifed and shot during a holdup because he had prayed to Malverde. Lacking any photographic evidence or contemporary description of his saint protector, González asked an artisan in the neighborhood to make up a face, drawing on those of a famous actor of the time and a local politician. The cult of Jesus Malverde, which has grown steadily since the 1970s, is especially popular among drug traffickers, pickpockets, and the marginalized and endangered of the night, including prostitutes, bar owners, and taxi drivers.

Sometimes, Malverde the "narco-saint" will be paired on the same altar with a gruesome image of a skeleton, typically dressed in a long robe and carrying a scythe and a globe. This is *La Santa Muerte* or Saint Death, also known as "The Little Skinny

One," whose cult has grown wildly in the last decade or so to include more than 2 million followers in northern Mexico and the United States, among, as one might guess, those same marginalized groups that cluster around Malverde, and for whom death is a preoccupation. The evil twin to Our Lady of Guadalupe, *Santa Muerte* does a wide variety of shady work for those who pray to her, including protecting them from violent death, helping them find hidden money, and, for women with wayward lovers, acting as cupid's enforcer—with her scythe. When dressed in a black robe and coupled with a black candle, Saint Death can be called upon to perform the most distasteful black magic, and so it is not surprising that she and Malverde have both been condemned by the Mexican Catholic Church. Indeed, it has long been rumored that human sacrifice is part of *La Muerte*'s belief package and ritual, and on March 30, 2012, a family of eight of her followers was arrested by the Sonora State Police for having allegedly killed a 55-year-old woman and two ten-year-old boys; according to the police, their throats and wrists were slit and their blood spread on the saint's altar. Of course *La Santa Muerte* has no historical basis, and while Jesus Malverde was a real person, his CV is so thoroughly unwholesome that his cult lies well outside the boundaries of the Catholic litany of saints, converging instead with the hero cult of ancient Greece, where the greatest hero of all, Herakles, was forced to accomplish his Twelve Labors in order to redeem himself for having killed his first wife and three children.

Elvis demonstrated the possession of Weber's charisma long before his premature death, through his initial phenomenal success as an entertainer in the mid '50s. This gift he had in effect earned, through his own unprecedented on-stage and record-industry performance. (For Michael Jackson, the equivalent period of charismatic ascent came in the early '80s, following his phenomenally successful 1982 *Thriller* album and his signature Moonwalk, whose epiphany before 47 million viewers came shortly thereafter, on the TV special *Motown 25: Yesterday, Today, Forever*.) The then-new medium of television played a critical role for Elvis, whose charismatic potential, in the later '50s, was multivalent and not fully realized. Like Simeon, Elvis was doing something extraordinary and unprecedented and, for some, disturbing and abnormal. Both became the object of wide-spread attention and both, at a young age, were elevated above the normal to the status of

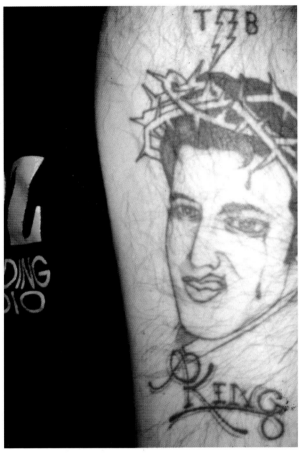

FIG. 8

charismatic. And as difficult as it was to gain that pedestal, it was, ironically, not at all easy to fall back down to the mundane, despite drug addiction and, for Jackson, charges of child molestation. Through the dismal movie years of the '60s and the increasingly degenerate Vegas years of the '70s, and even as Elvis became bloated and dazed and began to forget the lines to his familiar songs, he remained endowed by his fans with inalienable charisma.

Clearly, Elvis was one of Max Weber's charismatics, but he was and remains more than that. Within the conventional typology of Christian saints, comprising martyrs, ascetics, and confessors, Elvis, in the eyes of his ardent fans, has his place as a martyr. Followers emphasize Elvis's profound spiritualism and his painful, premature death—a death described as coming at the hands not of the evil Dr. Nick, but of his own fans, whose merciless demands for Elvis entertainment exhausted and ultimately killed Elvis the entertainer. He was, in effect, forced to take uppers to prepare for a concert and then downers to get the necessary rest in preparation for the next one. In their eyes, as evidenced by their inscriptions and their iconography (fig. 8), Elvis had died for them, and any further revelations of his seeming debauchery would only reconfirm and intensify their image of his Christ-like suffering.

A charismatic who suffers an unjust, early death is well on his or her way to secular sainthood; a violent death is even more effective in achieving that outcome. Indeed, the litany of secular charismatic martyrs to which Elvis belongs is rich and varied. Michael Jackson's meteoric rise and tragic fall is a match for Elvis; moreover, his death has officially been classified as a homicide, as Elvis's never was. Michael's death, though not violent in a conventional sense, was no less unjust than was that of Father Karastamatis of Santa Cruz, who was brutally murdered in his own parish. Ernesto Che Guevara was another such victim, though in his case, martyrdom came not at the hands of his personal physician or a crazed Satanist, but rather, at the behest of the CIA, operating though Bolivian anti-revolutionary guards. As Che championed the cause of South America's poor and died for it, Martin Luther King, Jr., clearly another charismatic martyr, championed the cause of America's blacks and died for it, and Harvey Milk championed the cause of America's gays and died for it. In each case, there is the powerful mix of a charismatic personality, a cause, a struggle, and an unjust, violent early death—and, of course, devoted followers pre- and postmortem.

The fact that Harvey Milk was Jewish did not inhibit the GLBT Historical Society SoMa ("South of Market") from laying out the clothes in which he was assassinated, with their bullet holes, in the shape of a cross, as part of their December 2008 exhibition *Passionate Struggle: Dynamics of San Francisco's GLBT History*, nor did it stop Brother Robert Lent, Order of Friars Minor, from making an icon of him (fig. 9), as he had already done for Bob Marley, Martin Luther King, Jr., Caesar Chavez, and others. According to the website of the icon's vendor, Trinity Stores:

> In this icon [Harvey Milk] holds a candle, keeping vigil himself for the oppressed of the world. He wears a black armband with a pink triangle. This was the Nazi symbol for homosexuals and represents all those who have been tortured or killed because of cultural fears regarding human sexuality. ...Christ continues to say, "As long as you did it to one of the least of these, you did it to Me."

Although she did not champion a social cause as lofty as South America's poor, America's blacks, or San Francisco's gay community, Selena Quintanilla-Pérez, variously known as the "Mexican Madonna" and the "Queen of Tejano Music," suffered a violent, early death at age 23—in her case, from a bullet fired by the president of her fan club, Yolanda Saldívar. Selena was a charismatic performer along the lines of Elvis and Michael Jackson, and, like Che Guevara, Martin Luther King, Jr., and Harvey Milk, she became the focus for self-identity and pride during her lifetime for a marginalized population—in her case, for America's burgeoning Hispanic

HARVEY MILK of SAN FRANCISCO

FIG. 9

community. The cover of the *Texas Monthly* of April 2010, published exactly 15 years after Selena's murder, bears an iconic image of the pop star with a thoroughly Catholic flavor appropriate to her fan base, wherein the banner with her name is carried by a white dove and Selena wears with a golden halo and holds her saintly attribute, a white rose, whose falling pedal substitutes for a saintly tear.

While no one would confuse Elvis, Michael Jackson, or Selena with those three murdered crusaders (Guevara, King, Milk), all were and are revered by their followers for their dedication to worthy causes. The Guinness World Records lists Michael Jackson under "Most Charities Supported by a Pop Star" for his contributions to 39 international organizations; during her lifetime, Selena would visit schools to promote the value of education, while in death, her Selena Foundation is dedicated to helping children in crisis; and at Graceland, a prominent section of the Trophy Building is devoted to documenting Elvis's legendary gift-giving, including donations to dozens of charities documented through the incontrovertible evidence of his cancelled checks. But despite their basic similarities, these three prematurely dead charismatic entertainers differ in one important respect, for while Selena was killed through no fault of her own by a crazed fan (who happened to be embezzling from her fan club), Elvis and Michael Jackson were both complicit in their deaths, insofar as both died from the soporific effects of drugs they themselves begged for. In fact, as we have already seen, this only adds another layer of angst for their followers. Certainly, they can blame Dr. George (Nick) Nichopoulos or Dr. Conrad Murry and, to some extent, most do. But without the smoking gun of the CIA/Bolivian guards, James Earl Ray, Dan "Twinkie Defense" White or, in Selena's case, the hateful Yolanda Saldívar, the arc of guilt turns back on themselves, the friends and fans, exposing their own failure to intervene, either directly for those who were close at hand (the Memphis Mafia—the Jackson family), or indirectly for everyone else who devoured their idols with their selfish demands for yet another dose of their charisma.

Elvis's Saint-Like Characteristics
Miracles

Miracle-working was part of the charisma package that came with Christian saints like Simeon; this, after all, was what they were expected to do, as Jesus had done, as proof of their special gifts. Simeon performed a wide variety of miracles from the top of his column: he restored the productivity of a farmer's field, stopped a plague of rats and mice, repelled man-eating wild animals, put water back in a dry spring, and preserved ships at sea. He could heal with his words, he could heal with his touch, and he could even heal with the dirt at the base of his column, which was believed to be infused with the saint's charismatic powers by way of contact—saint to column, column to hill. The blind were made to see, the lame were made to walk, and those possessed of demons (presumably, the mentally ill) were exorcised. Happily, these outcomes could be achieved anywhere, including for people who had never even paid Simeon a visit, by way of the saint's portable, charismatic dirt. But on a less dramatic level, Simeon was a healing power for the spirit, bringing peace to the troubled and clarity to the confused, either on site, through his comforting words delivered during his lifetime, or after death, through prayer, anywhere.

The charisma of Elvis, the superhuman entertainer, included miracle-working as one of its various potentialities, one of its possible "exceptional powers" (Weber's

characterization). Gradually, Elvis, together with his inner circle, began to culti-
vate those latent spiritual and miraculous potentialities, unconsciously drawing,
no doubt, on the laying-on-of-hands Pentecostal tradition from which Elvis and
many of his followers came. Eventually, the charismatic, pre-martyr Elvis became
an acknowledged healer. Larry Geller, Elvis's hairdresser and spiritualist, discusses
some typical manifestations of the King's miraculous powers of healing through
touch in his 1989 book *If I Can Dream: Elvis' Own Story*. He claims that Elvis once
healed a man having a heart attack and treated one of the Memphis Mafia, Jerry
Shilling, after a motorcycle accident: "The next thing I knew," Jerry said later, "I
woke up the following morning healed." In the '70s, claims Geller, concertgoers by
the hundreds brought their sick and crippled children to the stage, begging Elvis to
touch and hold them. Later in the same book, Geller captures through a quote from
Elvis a strange incident that in effect provides a theological explanation for his healing powers:

> In Elvis' mind, his life was being directed divinely.... And he truly felt
> that he was chosen to be here now as a modern-day savior, a Christ.
> [Elvis recounts:] 'Think back when I had that experience in the desert.
> I didn't only see Jesus' picture in the clouds—Jesus Christ literally
> exploded in me. Larry, it was me! I was Christ.'

With the layering on of martyrdom, Elvis dead became an ever more potent
miracle worker than Elvis living. Some of Elvis's posthumous miracles were gathered by clinical psychiatrist Raymond A. Moody, Jr. in *Elvis: After Life*, and these
are supplemented from time to time by the tabloids—even decades after the King's
death. Elvis appears to a small-town policeman, helping him locate his runaway son
by revealing a vision of the Los Angeles rooming house where, in fact, the boy turns
up a few days later. Elvis receives into paradise a young girl dying of complications
from Down's syndrome, just as she utters her last words: "Here comes Elvis!" Elvis
appears to a woman in the wood grain of her pantry door; Elvis waves to an old girlfriend though the miraculous movement of the sleeve of a jacket that he had once
given her.

In demonstrating his exceptional powers, Elvis the martyr most often takes on the role of Elvis the confessor. Moody relates the story of a clinical psychologist who, at a particularly low point in her life, is working late one night on a research paper. Looking up, she sees Elvis sitting in her patient's chair, asking with a kind smile: "Are you satisfied with your life, Missy?" A conversation ensues wherein Elvis is now the therapist, leaving Missy with a new-found sense of purpose and comfort. Words and images at Graceland, on Elvis graveside votives and on the Fans' Memorial Wall, tell a similar story. A heart-shaped flower arrangement in memory of Marie, "The Biggest French Elvis Fan," features a photo montage evoking the comforting presence of Elvis just over the deceased's left shoulder, while Shannon, on the Wall (fig. 10), testifies to the active, inspiring presence of Elvis in her life, as the King, through her sketch, looks on: "Elvis, You have inspired me in so many ways. Graceland is as beautiful as you described. LOVE, Shannon xoxo."

These are not the dramatic miracles of restored sight or replaced limbs; rather, these are the gentle, very personal miracles of postmortem, private epiphany, with resultant comfort and guidance. Not only can Elvis miraculously reveal himself in the gain of wood on a pantry door, he can weep through his image. For centuries, sacred pictures all over the world have appeared to shed real tears from time to time. On December 6, 1985, the Feast Day of Saint Nicholas, a large icon of the Virgin and Child in the Albanian Orthodox Church of St. Nicholas on the northwest side of Chicago began to weep; soon, to accommodate the enormous crowds of pious visitors, volunteers had to make the church available day and night,

FIG. 10

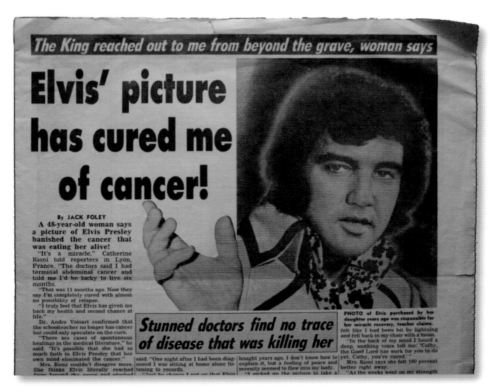

The King reached out to me from beyond the grave, woman says

Elvis' picture has cured me of cancer!

By JACK FOLEY

A 48-year-old woman says a picture of Elvis Presley banished the cancer that was eating her alive!

"It's a miracle," Catherine Rioni told reporters in Lyon, France. "The doctors said I had terminal abdominal cancer and told me I'd be lucky to live six months.

"That was 11 months ago. Now they say I'm completely cured with almost no possibility of relapse.

"I truly feel that Elvis has given me back my health and second chance at life."

Dr. Andre Voisart confirmed that the schoolteacher no longer has cancer but could only speculate on the cure.

"There are cases of spontaneous healings in the medical literature," he said. "It's possible that she had so much faith in Elvis Presley that her own mind eliminated the cancer."

Mrs. Rioni couldn't disagree more. She thinks Elvis literally reached

Stunned doctors find no trace of disease that was killing her

said. "One night after I had been diagnosed I was sitting at home alone listening to records.

bought years ago. I don't know how to explain it, but a feeling of peace and serenity seemed to flow into my body.

"I picked up the picture to take a

PHOTO of Elvis purchased by her daughter years ago was responsible for her miracle recovery, teacher claims.

felt like I had been hit by lightning and fell back in my chair with a moan.

"In the back of my mind I heard a deep, soothing voice tell me: 'Cathy, the Good Lord has work for you to do yet. Cathy, you're cured.'"

Mrs. Rioni says she felt 100 percent better right away.

"As the weeks went on my strength

FIG. 11

working in 12-hour shifts. This startling event made the tabloids as did, about three years later, the story of a weeping picture of Elvis, which was verified by a "stunned scientist" who "witnesses [the] incredible phenomenon with his own eyes."

Elvis mostly comforts and guides through his image, but sometimes he heals. "Elvis' Picture Has Cured Me of Cancer!" shouts the headline in the *Weekly World News* on December 29, 1987, as doctors are "stunned" (fig. 11). The gentle beginning of another Elvis miracle, with a clearly biblical flavor, was documented about that time in the *Elvis Fever Fan Club Quarterly* from Baltimore, under the heading: "Report from Memphis." The reporter relates how she and her friends, on the night of the candlelight vigil, witnessed an extraordinary celestial event as they waited opposite Graceland until after midnight to get in line for the walk-up to graveside. She and her sister noticed that there was only one star in the sky and that it was directly over Elvis' grave: "Understand this was the third year that this has occurred. It gave you an eerie feeling." Further endorsement of Elvis the miracle-worker came in *The New York Times* in 1995, in the Sunday *Magazine* lead article of September 24 by Ron Rosenbaum, titled "ELVIS HEALER." Rosenbaum notes with some astonishment and clear disdain that Elvis postmortem is attracting the hurt and the lame, who "find in the legacy of a fat, pill-filled Vegas singer, a healing power."

Relics

The word relic, which derives from the Latin verb "to leave behind" or "to relinquish," is usually understood to mean some physical remain from a martyr. One thinks immediately of the corpses of saints that fill French and Italian churches, mostly but not always behind slabs of marble, or of the various pieces of those corpses, which are most commonly bones or bone fragments, teeth or hair, which are often contained in, and occasionally visible within, sumptuous gold and silver reliquaries. A special category of such containers are called "speaking reliquaries," because the reliquary takes the shape of and thus "speaks for" the body part from which the relic originates; usually these are heads or arms.

But there is much more to relics than that, since Jesus himself left no bodily remains—provided one discounts such doubtful candidates as the various Holy Foreskins that have wandered Europe since the time of Charlemagne, one of which was paraded through the streets of the Italian village of Calcata on January 1, 1983, the Feast Day of the Circumcision. Since the early centuries of Christianity, the word relic has encompassed not only the whole or partial remains of sacred bodies but also any variety of things those sacred bodies had touched, and things that in turn had touched the things those sacred bodies had touched (Frazer's magical thinking: "the law of contact"). Jesus's body lay on the slab of limestone just to the right as one enters his Tomb shrine in Jerusalem; dirt or oil touching that slab and then carried out conveys with it the sacred power of the relic it touched and, at one remove, the power of Jesus. Jesus is nailed to the cross and the cross—the True Cross—is sanctified; the hole in which the cross was set, in the floor of Calvary Chapel in the Church of the Holy Sepulchre, by virtue of its having touched the cross, is likewise a relic. Base material like dirt and oil that comes in contact with that hole is believed infused with the miracle-working charisma of the cross and, by extension, of Jesus.

Each of these relics is part of a chain of objectified charisma, whose successive links are held together by contagion, seemingly without limit. Gregory, bishop of Tours in the later 6th century, tells of receiving from a pilgrim just back from Jerusalem a small silk robe that the pilgrim claimed had once wrapped a piece of the True Cross. Gregory was doubtful, but "dared" to wash the robe and give the wash water to the sick, who drank it and were healed. Amazed, he cut off pieces of the fabric and gave them to monks, who in turn used them to heal; an abbot reported back to Gregory that his scrap healed "twelve possessed people, three blind people, and two paralytics."As researchers have discovered, people are willing to pay a much higher price for a celebrity's sweater if they are convinced it had in fact been worn by the celebrity—and had never been washed.

The Holy Sepulchre and the True Cross were and remain star relics of Christ, though over the centuries there have been hundreds more of lesser renown. An anonymous pilgrim from Piacenza, in northern Italy, kept a diary as he made his journey through the Holy Land, around the year 570. He describes scores of Jesus contact relics, most of which have since been lost or destroyed. He is shown, in what is now the modern Israeli town of Zippori, the chair in which the Virgin sat during the Annunciation; in Nazareth, he sees the book in which the young Jesus learned his ABCs, in Cana, the jugs that had contained the water that Jesus miraculously turned to wine; in the Church of Holy Sion in Jerusalem, the column that Jesus clung to during the Flagellation; and just east of the Holy City, in the sand on the Ascension Mount, the imprint of Christ's feet.

Had the Piacenza pilgrim stopped at the hilltop shine of Saint Simeon on his way to the Holy Land, he undoubtedly would have been dazzled by the huge, cross-shaped church that had been erected around the column since the death of the saint, more than a century earlier, and by the enormous crowds of pilgrims that were housed nearby in the shrine's many hostels and at its large campground. He would not, however, have been shown the bodily remains of the saint, since they were carried away 40 miles or so to the nearest large city, Antioch, just days after the saint died. The Piacenza pilgrim would likely have heard from the local clergy at the shrine the dramatic story of Simeon's death: how a trusted disciple found his body cold, in *rigor mortis*, atop the column, and how he kept the news from the crowds below until a regional contingent of the Byzantine army could come to escort the body away.

For the Piacenza pilgrim the implication of this story would have been obvious: Simeon's disciple feared that the throng of Simeon followers at the base of his column would rip his body apart for relics—or that a group among them would conspire to steal the body whole. No, this was not to happen; Simeon was far too famous and his relics too important to be dispersed that way, and in fact, the patriarch of nearby Antioch was set upon securing the saint whole, for his own town. So strong were his feelings that when he was later asked by the Byzantine emperor that Simeon's bones be "translated" (ceremonially transferred) to Constantinople, he had the temerity to refuse, noting that Constantinople had fortified walls to protect it, whereas all Antioch had for protection were the bones of Simeon. The Piacenza pilgrim may even have heard the story of the unfortunate bishop who snipped off a piece of Simon's cloak for himself, just as the saint's body reached the ground, only to be shocked to discover that the offending hand had withered with leprosy. So in the end, Antioch was to have the saintly body of Simeon, and there oil could be passed through his tomb and over his bones in order to generate relics for the visiting faithful. By contrast, *Qal`at Sem`ān* ("Castle of Simeon"), as the hilltop shrine of Saint Simeon later came to be called, was to have the saintly column, and the charismatic dirt of the hill upon which it stood.

The chaotic scene at Simeon's column on that day in early September 459 when its resident charismatic made his exit is easily imagined: as the dead body of Simeon is lowered from the top of his column, the crowd surges forward, struggling to break through the protective barrier of Byzantine soldiers, to touch the saintly remains, and perhaps take a piece of clothing. Now, fast forward to the '50s, and envision the chaotic scene as Elvis struggles to escape his crazed fans after a concert. Screaming teenage girls break through, ripping Elvis' clothing, scratching his flesh. Prized relics of the emerging King of Rock 'n' Roll are spirited away. Then fast forward again, but this time to the '70s, as Elvis reemerges on tour after a decade of movie making. Now the Elvis version of Simeon's Byzantine soldiers—the Memphis Mafia, working with local police—make sure that Elvis escapes the building intact. Now, the distribution of cloth contact relics is institutionalized in the form of the multiple scarves hastily draped over Elvis' sweaty neck by his on-stage handlers and almost as quickly passed on by Elvis to adoring fans at stage-side. The concert finale, by comparison to the '50s, is predictable and orderly, coming after the signature last song—*Can't Help Falling in Love*—with the signature statement of closure: "Ladies and gentlemen, Elvis has left the building." The scrap of Elvis gold lamé suit from 1957, the Elvis sweaty scarf from 1977, and fragment of Simeon the Stylite's hair shirt from 459 are all, at their most basic level, the same: relics empowered by contact with an acknowledged charismatic. And although the *vitae* of Simeon do not relate any miracle accomplished by way of his clothing (aside from the would-be thief's withered hand), such miracles certainly took place, given the frequency with which he accomplished contagion miracles with his touch and with the dirt at the base of his column. Similarly, Raymond A. Moody, Jr. in *Elvis: After Life* describes a miracle wherein a jacket once worn by Elvis spontaneously waves at the girl to whom he gave it from the closet where it was hanging.

Elvis relics, like those of other secular charismatics of our day, are valued and traded. On October 18, 2009, Leslie Hindman Auctioneers of Chicago put on the block more than 200 items from the Gary Pepper (deceased Elvis friend and fan club president) Collection of Elvis Presley Memorabilia, including a clump of hair said to have been retrieved from the barbershop floor on that fateful day, March 25, 1958, when the soon-to-be Private Elvis had his locks cut in the Fort Chaffee, Arkansas, barbershop; exceeding expectations, it fetched $15,000, while a shirt that once belonged to the King went for $52,000. Too expensive? With a few strokes of the computer keyboard, anyone can wander the cyber-shops of *eBay* and discover much cheaper pre-packaged strands of Elvis hair and patches of Elvis clothing: a short strand of hair trades in the $40 range, while a small square of a dress shirt Elvis is said to have once worn is closer to $60 (fig. 12). As for Elvis signatures, a simple reprint goes for just $5, whereas an "Elvis Presley Signed Vintage B/W Photo GAI Autograph"—an apparently original Elvis signature on a publicity photo for his 1962 movie *Follow that Dream*—is

FIG. 12

trading in the $1,000 range. The trade names of those selling bits of Elvis hair and clothing—Rock 'n' Roll Relics and Celebrity Threads—may do little to reassure a skeptical buyer of authenticity, though such assertive phrases as "Authentic Elvis Worn" might, or perhaps the signed attestation on the back of the package will. On the other hand, those who are prepared to believe that the face of Elvis is revealed in statuary of Pharaoh Amenhotem IV are likely to be persuaded by vials of "Elvis' Sweat!" as well, whose seller's passing engagement with the authenticity question is confined to the tongue-in-cheek affirmation: "ABSOLUTELY contains a few *precious* drops of Elvis' perspiration. SERIOUSLY."

At the other extreme of endorsement is Global Authentication Inc. (GAI), invoked on *eBay* in the sale of the signed Elvis photo from *Follow that Dream*. Global Authentication, in the words of its website "provides unique solutions to dealers, collectors and corporations by integrating state of the art consumer protection technology and world class grading/authentication experts to Sports, Historical and Hollywood memorabilia." For someone ready to spend $1,000 on a signed Elvis photo, that is probably very comforting, as long as the buyer ignores or fails to find the story via *Google* in the November 8, 2007, *Sports Collectors Daily*, reporting that GAI, according to a government official in San Clemente, California, had been operating there without a license and had vacated its building "in a hurry." When it comes to blue-chip security for the trade in Elvis relics, the analogue to Christie's and Sotheby's is Jerry Osborne's *Presleyana* series, which is now up to *Volume VI*, in print and on line. The list of offerings is dense, the descriptions crisp. Under the category of "shoes" is an entry for pumps, 1956, manufactured by the Faith Shoe Company, and put up for sale by the estate—that is, Elvis Presley Enterprises, Inc. A pair of pumps that Elvis wore in 1956, still in their box, is valued at $2,800, whereas a single Elvis shoe of that era, without its box, can be had for $1,000.

Icons

To be a saint is to have icons. The icon is the legacy of Byzantium (AD 330-1453), the Christian, East Roman Empire governed out of Constantinople. In Greek, the word *eikon* simply means "image," and today it is usually understood to mean an abstract religious portrait painted in egg tempera on a gold-covered wooden board.

But an icon could also be a mosaic or even a coin; it could be elaborate or simple, one of a kind or mass produced. What defined an icon in Byzantium (and among Orthodox Christians to this day) was neither medium nor style but rather how the image was used and, especially, what people believed it to be. Thus, much like Max Weber's charismatic, the icon was and is affectively defined: it exists in the eye of the beholder. Icons could, therefore, appear miraculously in natural phenomena, like clouds and the bark of trees, provided, of course, they were recognized and acknowledged. In the 15th century, an icon of the Virgin and Child with John the Baptist was discovered in the Rorschach veining of a slab of marble in Byzantium's greatest church, Hagia Sophia, more than 900 years after the church was built.

An icon is a devotional image, deserving of special reverence and respect. This is so because an icon is believed to share in the sanctity of the figure whose likeness it bears. The accepted Orthodox view was succinctly stated nearly 12 centuries ago by Saint Theodore of the Studion Monastery:

> Every artificial image...exhibits in itself, by way of imitation, the form of its model...the model [is] in the image, the one in the other, except for the difference of substance.

Christ and his icon, the model and its image, are one, yet the divinity of Christ remains distinct from the wood and paint of the panel. From the point of view of its devotional use, the panel as a physical thing therefore disappears, as in the eyes of the faithful it becomes one and the same with what it portrays. It becomes, in effect, a window or door through which one gains access to the sacred figure portrayed.

When a Byzantine Christian stood before an icon of Christ or a saint, he believed himself literally to be standing before the figure portrayed; for him, this place of encounter was a sacred place. Frontality and direct eye contact are essential in icons; references to earthly time or real space, in the background or to the sides, are both distracting and irrelevant to the icon's purpose. A neutral (typically, gold) background, bust-length format, over-large eyes, gestures of communication, and a general sense of timelessness are defining characteristics of icons. The purpose of this intense focus and compositional simplicity was to concentrate and thereby enhance the potential for the image mystically to bring the figure portrayed into the presence of the viewer. Full-frontal images of Saint Simeon's face impressed into the dirt from his hilltop shrine were instrumental in bringing the saint's healing presence to those who could not make it to the shrine itself during Simeon's lifetime, and to anyone after the saint's death. Once the saint was "there" (spiritually on site) he could perform his miracles via that very dirt.

FIG. 13

An icon not only brought the saint, it was designed to facilitate spiritual dialogue. Consider the extraordinary 6th- to 7th-century icon of Christ in the Monastery of Saint Catherine at Mount Sinai (fig. 13). A Byzantine text from around 1200 describing just such an iconic image of Christ provides the key to understanding its use: "His eyes are joyful and welcoming to those who are not reproached by their conscience." The face of this icon combines two very different moods and thereby facilitates two very different directions for dialogue. The left ("sinister") side of Christ's face would certainly attract the attention of those "reproached by their conscience": the eyebrow is arched, the lip and mustache are drawn down almost in a sneer, and the overall effect is clearly threatening. By contrast, the proper right side of Christ's face is benign to the point of sweetness, creating a "joyful and welcoming" impression for "those who are not reproached by their conscience." Depending on your mental state, the icon could engage you very differently.

An icon is defined not only by what it looks like and what it is designed to help you do, but also by what it does all by itself. As icons offer a door to mortals to gain access to the divine, so also they offer a channel going the other direction, bringing heavenly power down to earth. The story of miracle-working icons goes back to the 6th century, to the time of the Piacenza pilgrim. There was a second, "younger" Saint Simeon the Stylite, who was an imitator of the first; he was resident on a column in northern Syria not far from the "elder" Simeon's column, though about 150 years later. In the *vita* of this younger Simeon, there is a report of a miracle-working icon as well as a theological explanation for how that icon got its healing power. A barren woman possessed by a demon is exorcised by this second Saint Simeon; she

FIG. 14

returned home, conceived, and delivered a child:

> [then] ... she put up the image
> of the saint inside her house,
> and this image performed
> miracles, because the Holy Spirit
> which inhabited Simeon covered
> it with its shadow....

The power of the Holy Spirit was not only in the saint, it overshadowed the saint's icon as well, much as the Holy Spirit overshadowed the Virgin Mary in the Annunciation.

A glance around the gift shops opposite Graceland Manson is revealing; air-brushed away to a stark simplicity, Elvis icons stare forth in multiples from the walls (fig. 14), matching in their intensity the icons of early Byzantium from which they seem to descend. Images of Elvis like these are best suited to facilitating the gentle miracles described above, wherein Elvis appears to comfort and guide. Like Byzantine icons, they bring the figure portrayed into the spiritual presence of the viewer and facilitate a dialogue. But icons also have the power to do much more dramatic things, like repel arrows and save cities. According to the tabloids, an Elvis picture could not only weep, it could even cure cancer. Moreover, testimony recorded in Moody's *Elvis: After Life* describes yet another category of Elvis icon miracle, wherein his image is suddenly recognized by a fan in the wood grain of an old pantry door—much as the image of Christ was recognized five centuries earlier in the veining of a marble slab in Hagia Sophia.

One medium for Elvis portraiture carries its own powerful, affective meaning for Elvis fans, namely, velvet. In late January 2010, after four years of much notoriety and some ridicule, Velveteria, the one and only velvet painting museum, in Portland, Oregon, closed its doors. Its 300-plus paintings on velvet were a monument to a peculiar medium that seems to have reached its apogee in Tijuana in the '70s. Elvis pictures have been so prevalent in this medium that they have their own term of identification: an Elvis on velvet is a Velvis. Why the association? Is it simply because velvet painting is *ipso facto* a genre of high kitsch art and for many Elvis Presley is the essence of kitsch? This may explain some of the association, but probably not all of it. Think of what dominates the iconography of velvet painting besides Elvis, sultry

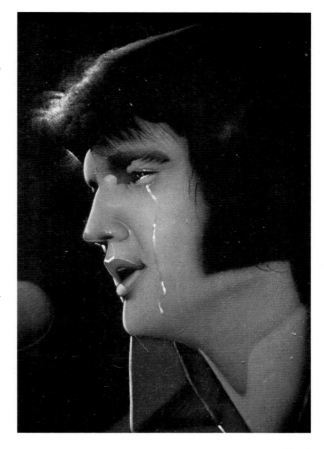

FIG. 15

Polynesian nudes, and insipid unicorns. This is an art form for charismatic martyrs, including Jesus, JFK, MLK, Michael Jackson, and Che Guevara, and for various incarnations of sad big-eyed waifs, clowns, and puppies. And everywhere possible in velvet art are tears.

The descent from canvas to velvet is the descent from pathos to bathos. With their dark, dramatic backgrounds and sketchy, ambiguous details, paintings on velvet are powerful agents for opening the emotional floodgates of susceptible viewers. Moreover, they have a comforting, tactile quality. As neuroscientists have recently discovered, our visual brain will complete the compositional and emotional ambiguity of works of art to suit our own sensibilities. This is part of the work and the joy of viewing art. The process applies universally, whether the work in question is a half-finished landscape by Cezanne or a simple sketch of the partially averted face of a child by Rembrandt—or a Velvis showing the King in concert, where Elvis sweat and Elvis (imagined) tears seem to meld (fig. 15). As our visual brain will complete Cezanne's half-finished *Mont Ste. Victoire,* it will impute tender emotion to the ambiguous facial expression in the Rembrandt sketch—and the sweating (now weeping) Elvis on velvet will be empowered by our mental workings to both capture and evoke a profound sense of compassion and pity. Interestingly, the Elvis concert photo from which this Velvis derives was used on the cover of an album of Elvis ballads featuring his rendition of *Crying in the Chapel.* The velvet artist accentuated Elvis blue eyes and eliminated all the sweat, leaving only what appears to be a single large tear. As an Elvis icon is created to enable viewers to make conversational contact with the King, a Velvis is created to enable viewers to tap into their most profound emotions about the King. The comparable genre of northern European art of the later Middle Ages was called the *Andachsbilt* ("devotional image"). By exaggerating the wounds and suffering of Christ and the grief of his mother Mary, German artists, especially, unleashed in devout viewers profound feelings of empathy. The Crown of Thorns Elvis tattoo lies somewhere between a German *Andachsbildt* and a Velvis; certainly, its emotive power would be even greater were its background not skin but velvet.

As a miracle-working charismatic martyr, Elvis differs from most of his counterparts, and from Christ and Saint Simeon, by virtue of the fact that his primary vehicle for making contact, for "being there," both pre- and postmortem, was and is his singing voice. True, music has always been an integral part of the Christian icon experience as well, but in reverse: believers sing to icons, not the other way around. Song is among the honorific acts that icons deserve, because they share in the sanctity of the figures they portray; icons also deserve incense and candles, and elaborate stands for display. All of these elements added together create a powerful, spiritual atmosphere that facilitates the icon's role in bringing the holy figure portrayed into the presence of the faithful for spiritual dialogue and, potentially, for miracles. Contrast this with the role of music in the Elvis cancer-healing miracle documented on the front page of the *Weekly World News* on December 29, 1987. The story involves a 48-year-old school teacher in Lyon, France, named Cathy:

> *One night after I had been diagnosed I was sitting at home alone listening to records. Just by chance I put on that Elvis song 'In the Ghetto' and glanced at a picture of him that my daughter bought years ago. I don't*

> know how to explain it, but a feeling of peace and serenity seemed to
> flow into my body. ... When my finger touched his face I felt like I had
> been hit by lightning and fell back in my chair with a moan. In the back
> of my mind I heard a deep, soothing voice tell me: 'Cathy, the Good Lord
> has work for you to do yet. Cathy, you're cured.'

The miracle is accomplished through a combination of song, image, and touch, in that order. Cathy is initially in a transformed state of "peace and serenity" as a result of an Elvis song and an Elvis picture working in tandem. Her finger seems to have a mind of its own, as it moves (is drawn) to touch the face of Elvis in his picture, and at that instant, peace and serenity are replaced by the impact of "lightning," which results in involuntary movement and a moan. Finally, Elvis appears through his voice, and performs his healing miracle.

Now, compare this with a healing miracle recorded in the *vita* of the younger Saint Simeon, in which the saint's image, impressed on his sacred dirt, accomplishes the iconic epiphany (the "being there") not with the powerful aid of music but rather with the powerful aid of incense—olfactory as opposed to aural. The story involves a priest whose son is half-dead and desperate. Together they pay a visit to Simeon and ask that he apply his healing right hand, which he does, but tells them to go home, assuring them that the boy will eventually be well. The doubtful priest is reluctant to leave, which annoys the saint, who scolds him for his lack of faith, but then reassures him that everything will be fine. Back home, just as one child recovers, another, the priest's youngest son, becomes desperately ill with chills and a fever. This child, too, wants to be taken to the saint but the priest is now confident that the saint can visit him at home and cure him through his earthen icon, which is the vehicle for the saint's subsequent epiphany:

> With these words...the young man gasps, falls into a trance, and cries
> out 'Saint Simeon, have pity on me.' Having spoken thus, he says to his
> father, 'Get up quickly, throw on incense, and pray, for the servant of
> God, Saint Simeon, is before me.'

The boy then falls silent for a long time, but eventually opens his eyes and recounts how Simeon has taken the demon that has afflicted the family to burn him in a furnace. Completing the dramatic narrative, the child once again is well, thanks to the saint's sacred dirt, his image impressed on it, and the incense. Clearly, this miracle and the Elvis cancer-curing miracle 15 centuries later have much in common.

For centuries, Russian Orthodox families have designated part of their home, however simple, as a special place for spiritual contemplation. It is the *Krasny Ugol*, which means both the "beautiful corner" and the "red corner." This will usually be the corner opposite the entrance, and thus the first one seen, and it is the location of the family's most important icons. Roman families had their equivalent, which was their *lararium* or "altar"; for wealthy families, the *lararium* was typically situated in the atrium, near the front door, whereas for families of lesser means, it would be near the hearth. This was where the family's collection of gods was kept—usually small statuettes—along with objects relating to the family history. It was their location for prayer, just like the *Krasny Ugol* was and remains for Russian families. Elvis fans "of the third level" often have their own version of such a domestic spot of solitude and spiritual contemplation, and they will call it their "Elvis Room." Most often this will be a made-over bedroom, though an Australian fan named Reg Penergast put on a 3000-square-foot addition to his home to accommodate all his "Elvis Stuff," and the phantasmagorical Granceland-like home of Paul MacLeod called Graceland Too (discussed in Section II) is one mega Elvis Room.

Elvis Rooms will usually be dominated by a multitude of mass-produced images of Elvis, perhaps including a Velvis like that in figure 15, for its emotive power, and Elvis icons of the sort illustrated in figure 14, for their utility in making spiritual contact with the King. Elvis Stuff will include kitschy tourist trinkets from Graceland Plaza, Elvis records, record jackets, books, and videos, juxtaposed with true relics, such as concert ticket stubs, Vegas sweat scarfs, original Elvis photographs, snapshots from multiple postmortem visits to Graceland, and, perhaps, an article or two of Elvis clothing. Ideally, there will be a CD player and/or a radio empowered with a subscription to Sirius Satellite Radio so that Elvis' singing voice can be channeled at will. And there may even be some expensive Elvis collectibles, like a full set of Elvis liquor music boxes made by the McCormick Distilling Company. Why? Because of the friendly rivalry among fans to demonstrate the depth of their individual Elvis devotion.

Vitae

To be a saint is to have not only icons but also *vitae,* which in Latin means "life and deeds." In a sense, it is the saint's biography, but a *vita* is very different from the typical sorts of biographies that are sold in a bookstore, including Guralnick's two monumental Elvis tomes. A saint's *vita* is anything but scholarly and dispassionate; on the contrary, a *vita* by definition freely interweaves historical truth and the miraculous, as if they partake in the same reality. Accuracy is not the aim. A *vita*'s author is typically a humble observer with special access to the saint and the intent is unabashedly propagandistic. A saint's *vita* was intended to convince those who read it or heard it read that the saint in question was a most extraordinary holy person, that he was more than worthy of emulation, veneration, and donations, and that his holy site certainly deserved a visit. (Then, as now, there was much competition for the attention, time, and wealth of the public; shrines were expensive to maintain and the towns that grew up around them depended on a pilgrimage economy.)

Saint Simeon the Stylite has three *vitae*, all written during his lifetime; they vary somewhat among themselves but, like the four Gospels, they tell basically the same story. Differences appear in details about, for example, the episode of the palm-frond rope around the waist. Where did Simeon find the rope? One *vita* says it was the rope from the bucket in the monastery's well. How long did he wear it? One source says just ten days, another, a full year. How was it discovered that young Simeon was mortifying his flesh in this bizarre way? One source says there was dripping blood, another, an intolerable stench. Typically, Simeon's three *vitae* combine facts—the saint did live on a column for 37 years, he did communicate by letter with Emperor Theodosius, he did die in 459—with fiction, or at least wishful thinking. Aside from the many implausible miracles recounted, there is the question of what any human being physically can do, no matter how spiritually motivated.

All Christian holy stories, beginning with the Gospels, draw on the formulaic life stories of ancient heroes and, like them, have a few predictable ingredients. There is often a special birth and some unusual distinction achieved at an early age: the beautiful Helen of Troy is hatched from an egg; the powerful Herakles vanquishes a snake as a child. The infant Jesus had the Star of Bethlehem to signal his birth and Elvis, as his *vita* reveals, was born on a night when a blue ring encircled the moon. Jesus was precocious, dazzling the religious leaders of Jerusalem with his wisdom at the age of 12. Similarly, Simeon distinguished himself as a teenager, not by his wisdom but by the fact that he could endure more self-inflicted pain than anyone else. As for Elvis, he stood out from his classmates as a ten-year-old when he sang *Old Shep* at the Mississippi-Alabama Fair and Dairy Show, dazzling the judges with his extraordinary voice.

There may be a point in the *vita* of epiphany or revelation—a point when the charisma or gift suddenly shines forth and is acknowledged. The Magi saw and acknowledged the divinity of the infant Jesus on what became the Feast of the Epiphany, January 6. Three decades later, John the Baptist re-recognized and baptized Jesus, launching his career of preaching and miracle-working. The role of John the Baptist for Elvis was played by Sun Records producer Sam Phillips, when he discovered and acknowledged his extraordinary singing talent and launched his career. It all unfolded in July 1954, when Elvis was just 19 years old. On July 5, Sam recorded Elvis singing *That's All Right*; soon thereafter, the demo was passed along to local deejay Dewey Phillips, who played it for the first time on station WHBQ on Saturday evening, July 10—by popular demand, 13 times in a row. Then, on July 30, Elvis performed for the first time at Overton Park in Memphis, and the teenage girls went wild. The rest is history.

Extraordinary birth, early distinction, and public epiphany are typically followed by the "good deeds" segment of the charismatic's life. For both Jesus and Simeon, this was the time of miracle-working and preaching. For Elvis, the years of great accomplishments were his high-performance music and movie years, extending from his summer 1954 epiphany on the radio and on stage to late 1973, with the finalization of his divorce from Priscilla and the beginning of his precipitous physical and mental decline. The successive phases and milestones of the 19-year arc are familiar: first, the rising rock 'n' roller and then the army private with, along the way, memorable TV appearances with Steve Allen and Ed Sullivan, and the death of mother Gladys in August 1958. Then the movie years of the '60s, when Elvis the stage and television performer was out of sight; in addition to 27 post-Army movies, highlights of this decade included his marriage to Priscilla on May 1, 1967, the birth of Lisa Marie exactly nine months later, and his last #1 record, *In the Ghetto,* in 1969. The next phase of Elvis' life, the touring and Vegas years of the '70s, was launched with his famous '*68 Comeback Special* and culminated in his *Elvis—Aloha from Hawaii* concert of January 1973, the first worldwide television broadcast seen by more than a billion people in 40 countries.

After good deeds and fame, the *vita*'s story line will typically turn to the saint's last days, which will often include a passion (suffering) and martyrdom (death), and sometimes includes as well posthumous epiphanies and/or miracles, as in the Gospels. For Christians, this is the Easter story leading up the Ascension. For Elvis fans, the King's "passion cycle" began in earnest in late 1973 when his divorce from Priscilla was finalized. Elvis' addiction and general deterioration accelerated after that until his death in August 1977; the video of his last public performance, at the Market Square Arena in Indianapolis on June 26 of that year, reveals Elvis bloated, dazed, and seemingly despondent, in the last throws of his public passion and on the threshold of his martyrdom.

There are more than 1,700 books about Elvis, many of which have some insider authorship. The vast majority have some *vita* flavor, though none among them captures the full Saint Elvis story in the way each of the three Simeon *vitae* does. The *This Is Elvis* documentary of 1981 presents the basic Elvis *vita* outline, which is complemented and embellished by most of the subsequent accounts. There is the humble birth scene in a shotgun shack in the poorest section of Tupelo, Mississippi, and the loss of his stillborn twin Jesse Garon, the first of many tragic losses for Elvis, including Gladys in 1958 and Priscilla in 1973. Elvis's early years are spare but happy, as the beloved only child of Gladys and Vernon, who are portrayed as good, simple, religious people, instilling in their son respect for God and his fellow man. Elvis's future career in entertainment and his lifelong acceptance of people of all races and backgrounds are anticipated by his youthful attention to and admiration for the poor but talented blacks across town who sing the blues on their porches. Young Elvis manifests his trademark humility and respect for adults by always helping out and taking care to address his elders with southern politeness, as "sir" and "ma'am." His desire to perform for others emerges early as well, as attested by a legendary episode in the Tupelo Hardware Co. on Elvis's ninth birthday, when he chooses a guitar over a bicycle as his present. Elvis is a devoted and affectionate son, later a loving husband and father, and always a loyal friend. He is surprised by his powerful impact on young women and by his meteoric rise to be the King of Rock 'n' Roll, but remains true to his roots through it all. His religion stays with him; his spirituality grows with the years. And there are not only painful losses in Elvis's life (Jesse Garon, Gladys, and Priscilla), and betrayals (Priscilla, a faction of his Memphis Mafia, and Dr. Nick), but also multiple, painful afflictions of the body (everything from glaucoma to an enlarged colon to cancer) that are exacerbated by his heroic commitment to entertain his fans. Life slips away, tragically, and millions mourn: Elvis dies and the nation weeps.

"He was the finest boy you'd ever want to know." This was the eloquent and passionate mantra of Jannette Fruchter, who lived with her husband Rabbi Alfred Fruchter and two children in a duplex above the Presleys at 462 Alabama Avenue in Memphis, when Elvis was a teenager, between the ages of 15 and 18. Alfred, whom Elvis called "Sir Rabbi," was the leader of the small Orthodox congregation where George Klein—who would later be Elvis's agent and close friend, and now his radio DJ—celebrated his *bar mitzvah*. The Presleys were then even poorer than the Fruchters, who lent Elvis their record player, helped their neighbors with their water bill, and invited them up for the Jewish Feast of Tabernacles (*Sukkah*) each fall. According to Janette, Elvis would turn over the paycheck from his after-school job at Crown Gas to his mother Gladys and would help her bring in the groceries she bought with his earnings. In the Fruchter household, Elvis was the *Shabbos goy*, the gentile who would turn on the lights for them on Friday nights and Saturdays when Orthodox Jews are forbidden to do so; he refused ever to take any money for his services. As for Elvis's later decline into drugs, Janette Fruchter was convinced it was because his mother, with whom he had been very close, died too young. "He was one of the biggest *menches* I've ever known," she said of Elvis.

All of these glowing character values are revealed in broad strokes in *This Is Elvis* through a mélange of news accounts, photographs, and videos of Elvis the performer and Elvis the man, and four different Elvis actors. What is missing, or at least not fully fleshed out in this 1981 documentary, are Elvis's miracles, Elvis's passion and martyrdom, Elvis's afterlife, and Graceland relics and postmortem rituals. All of these missing pieces were, however, individually addressed within the next several years. For miracles there are Raymond Moody's *Elvis After Life* and Larry Geller's *If I Can Dream* from 1987 and 1989; for Elvis's passion and martyrdom, May Mann's *Elvis: Why Don't They Leave You Alone* from 1982; for his afterlife, Gail Brewer-Giorgio's *Is Elvis Alive?* from 1986; and for relics and rituals there are Rosalind Cranor's *Elvis Collectibles* and Jane and Michael Stern's *Elvis World*, both from 1987. Layer on the tabloids and the composite Elvis *vita* is essentially complete about a dozen years after his death; by contrast, the Gospels took about 70 years to complete. Its flavor, distilled to its most extreme, is captured in the cancer-healing miracle on the front page of the *Weekly World News* and in the recreation by May Mann in her description of the King's final moments:

> *Elvis was seated on the toilet, actually reading a religious book...when suddenly a terrible pain gripped him in his stomach and seized his heart with a strangler's grip. 'Oh no, dear dear God,' he thought. He couldn't move. He couldn't get up. He had to get up.... That terrible pain, like swords of fire, jabbing, slitting, cutting into his stomach, and especially his liver—it was impossible to bear.... ...suddenly the thought flashed through him: this must be like what Jesus suffered.*

Of course, most Elvis *vita* literature was not intended to fill out the largely sympathetic 1981 documentary but rather to set the record straight on the "true Elvis," by refuting Albert Goldman's mean-spirited 1981 polemic, *Elvis*, wherein the reader learns, among many other gruesome details of Elvis's private life, that multiple daily injections of drugs left Elvis's flesh looking like a pincushion. In the typology of early Christian polemical writings, Goldman's book would be classified not as biography but as a *contra* ("attack"), as in *Contra Elvis*. It is a brutal attack on a cherished dead man and on his cherished memory, and it therefore needed to be refuted. In the typology of early Christian polemics, this category of refutation would be an *apologia*. The two, taken together, effectively constitute an argument. And to this day the Elvis *contra/apologia* argument is still being played out. Goldman makes the assertion—the attack—that Elvis died not of cardiac arrest brought on by a multiplicity of interacting chronic conditions (for May Mann, it was cancer that killed him), but rather from a self-administered, accidental overdose of prescription drugs. Dr. Nick, of course, is identified as the careless (or worse) enabler and earns the unenviable title of "The Man Who Killed Elvis." (In fact, Dr. Nick was indicted on 14 counts of over-supplying drugs to Elvis and other patients, including Jerry Lee Lewis.)

Finally, at the age of 83, and on the occasion of what would have been Elvis's 75th birthday, Dr. George Nichopoulos came forth with his own version of events leading up to August 16, 1977. This was Nick's *apologia,* or justification, of himself, but of Elvis as well. His aim, of course, was to clear his name, and he attempted to do so by painting a diagnostic picture of Elvis that is composed of an implausible abundance of ailments: diabetes, glaucoma, arthritis, gout, fatty liver, "bad stomach," enlarged heart, migraines, insomnia, constipation, oversized colon, and panic attacks. Add to this Elvis's life-long performance anxiety and his childish obsession with instant ("in a flash") gratification, and one ends up with the scores of pharmaceutical regimes that Dr. Nick and others were obliged to supply. It was not that any one of these drugs killed Elvis, asserts the doctor, or even that their interaction did him in; no, he was simply a very sick and worn out 42-year-old. And therefore, since it wasn't Dr. Nick's fault, it must have been Elvis's grueling regime of entertaining that aged him prematurely and made him sick in so many ways. This necessarily puts the burden of guilt where it belongs and always has belonged: squarely on the fans themselves. The evil Albert Goldman is rebuffed, George Nichopoulos is exonerated (how often he "struggled" to substitute a placebo), and Elvis, who likewise is exonerated from the label of "addict," becomes a martyr. A Goldman *contra* in 1981 and a Nichopoulos *apologia* in 2010—and perhaps finally, case closed.

As sympathetic recreations of Elvis gradually took written form, they became his composite *vita*, and the work goes on, as a new generation of fans combats Goldman's cynical successors in the ever-despised media. The local Memphis Mafia Fan Club, which still counts George Klein among its members, leaves no doubt about its "taking care of Elvis" mission in its graveside votive (fig. 16):

MOTTO:
We Take Care of Elvis' Legacy
& will never let anyone ever talk BAD
ABOUT HIM EVER
ELVISISTHEBOSS!!

Fans work to purge from Elvis's life history any references to drug abuse, obesity or paranoiac violence, speaking instead of a dirt-poor southern boy who rose to fame and glory, of the love of a son for his mother, of humility and generosity, and of

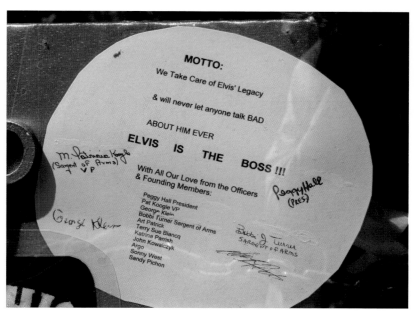

FIG. 16

superhuman achievement in the face of adversity. A fertile context for continuing postmortem Elvis elaboration in the good and right way are the annual Elvis Week "Conversations on Elvis" gatherings, where Elvis acquaintances from the past offer new tidbits each year to enrich his glowing life narrative. When necessary, facts are ignored or altered. For example, while it is known that Elvis was looking at pornography on the toilet when he was stricken with his drug-induced heart attack in his second-floor master bathroom, the saint-making story was soon promulgated, apparently from within Graceland itself, that what he had taken with him as reading material that morning was "a religious book on the Shroud of Turin."

The followers of charismatic martyrs, from the disciples of Jesus Christ to the revolutionaries of Che Guevara, have trouble letting go. How better to prove that Che was once and for all dead than by displaying his bullet-riddled body in that famous photo for all to see? Jim Morrison, the charismatic lead singer of the *The Doors*, was another martyr to drugs. Most believe that Morrison died in the bathtub of his Paris apartment on July 3, 1971, and that he was quickly and quietly buried five days later in Père Lachaise Cemetery. However, there were no photographs, no police report, and no autopsy, and so rumors persist that Jim had faked his death, "to escape." Tupac Shakur's die-hard hip-hop fans, 15 years after his unsolved murder, still refuse to accept that he is gone, despite the availability of his autopsy photographs on the Internet. Tupac recently "appeared" to an ecstatic crowd in a hologram-like apparition to perform at the Coachella Valley Music and Arts Festival in Indo, California. And now there are rumors that this hologram Tupac is going on tour, and that, with similar (actually, old and quite elementary) technology, John Lennon will again sing duets with Paul McCartney. But perhaps the most bizarre "not-dead" report is one with the dateline Baghdad. Five years after his death by hanging, on the occasion of what would have been his 74th birthday, Saddam Hussein was the subject of a YouTube video purporting to capture a recent telephone conversation between him and a member of the Iraqi Parliament; tellingly, the reporter for *The New York Times* characterized Hussein's various "still living" conspiracy theories as of the "Elvis variety."

It is easy to discount as absurd the notion that Elvis has lived before and/ or forever—that, for example, his identity is captured in the sculptures of Pharaoh Amenhotep IV, even though, to quote a *National Examiner* article of March 6, 1990, "Amenhotep worshipped the sun" and Elvis got his start recording at Sun Records. Even putting such absurdities aside, there remains much enthusiasm for the more mundane notion that Elvis is still living (fig. 17). There was near mania in the late '80s with the publication of Gail Brewer-Giorgio's *Is Elvis Alive?*, which came with an audio tape claiming to capture the post-1977 voice of the King. This was followed in 1991 and 1992 by two TV specials of the same title hosted by sometimes Elvis friend and *Speedway* costar Bill Bixby. One reported sighting was more bizarre than the next—Kalamazoo, Michigan, being the favorite for a while, given that it was the home of Rogaine and Elvis was, by that time, likely going bald.

The motivation theories then current were variously that Elvis simply wanted to escape his voracious fans, that he woke up to his obesity and drug problem and wanted to clean up his act, or that he had been an informant for the FBI in the war on drugs and had to fake his death and go into the witness protection program. Baptist minister Bill Beeny has spent nearly two decades letting the world know the "Elvis is Living" truth—a truth that he claims to have scientifically confirmed with a secret stash of Elvis DNA. The Beeny truth is that Elvis faked his own death to escape a Mafia hit and that the body in the casket viewed by thousands in the steaming heat of August 1977 was not Elvis but rather a rubber dummy. Benny's

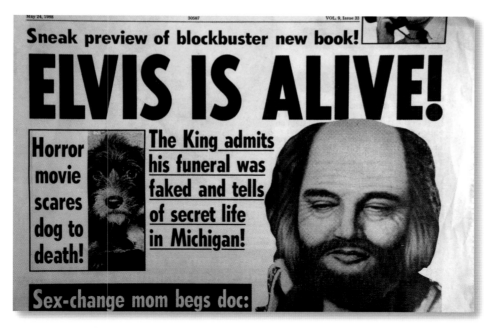

FIG. 17

print piece, *Final proof: The King IS alive!*, once available for $4, lists "100 facts why Elvis is alive," most of which rest on Beeny's novel approach to logic. At the time of his so-called death, Elvis weighed 255 pounds, says Beeny Fact #9, yet he had only two jumpsuits, even though he was about to go on tour: "Could it be he knew he would not need them?" The document concludes with an extra Fact, #101, asserting that 84% of the people questioned by Beeny believe Elvis to be alive.

Iconography

Jesus did not have the benefit, as did Elvis, of photography and video. Add to that the seemingly odd facts that the Gospel authors did not provide a physical description of their subject and that Jesus was never portrayed during his lifetime in any artistic medium, and one arrives at a simple but surprising truth: no one knows what Jesus looked like. Moreover, no one seems to have cared to give him a face in art for more than 250 years after his earthly life. Yes, Jesus was a Semite and yes, he was in his early 30s when he was crucified, but that is it; sandals, a toga, and a swarthy complexion do not make a portrait. It is no wonder that when Jesus was finally portrayed in art, around AD 300, sculptors and painters gave him the available forms of classical subjects: Jesus became the youthful, beardless Good Shepherd with a lamb over his shoulders; or the mature, curly-haired sun god with a magic wand in his hand; or the old, bearded philosopher carrying a book. It was only in the 6th century, in the age of the pilgrim from Piacenza, that Jesus at last is believed to have revealed his true image in the textiles that suddenly turned up miraculously imprinted, like the Shroud of Turin, with his contact "photo." This is the Jesus of the Sinai icon, which is substantially identical to Warner Sallman's Jesus on the basement wall of my childhood church.

Unlike Jesus, Elvis's true image was captured hundreds of thousands of times photographically; his face is recognized around the world. There was no invention needed, no Shroud of Turin-like miracles. Moreover, most Elvis icons are simply doctored Elvis photographs and not the creation of painters. What they share in common with icons of Jesus and the saints is their role in making a conversational connection between the viewer and the figure portrayed. Moreover, Elvis, like Jesus and all the saints, has iconography. These are figural artifacts—pictorial concoctions—that tell stories about their subject and, more importantly, express their creators' and viewers' shared beliefs about the subject; the icon of Harvey Milk is one such pictorial concoction.

Elvis iconography comes in many forms, from the divine to the mundane. Some years ago, *Parade Magazine* offered for sale an 18-inch-high polychrome statuette of Elvis, replete with a hand-tailored costume highlighted by more than 300 multicolored rhinestones. How do we recognize a Christian saint when we see one in art? By his iconography, which means by his facial type, by what he wears, by what attribute he holds, and sometimes, by what he is doing. A beardless young man in military dress with a sword at his waist and a lance in his hand: this is Saint Demetrios of Thessaloniki, an early 4th-century military saint, captured for eternity in a characteristic and recognizable form. In the Elvis iconography of the *Parade Magazine* statuette, the lance has turned into a microphone and the military garb into a jumpsuit, in order to evoke the King in one of his most characteristic manifestations: that of the famous *Elvis—Aloha from Hawaii* concert of 1973. Appropriately, the iconography is taken to the level of precise facial characterization; according to the accompanying text "the...face is painted by hand, bringing to life Elvis's noble profile, his soulful eyes, and his famous smile."

The iconography of saints typically mythologizes them in the same way that episodes in their *vita* do, combining the miraculous with the mundane. Elvis the martyr is evoked in a fan's tattoo where he is shown wearing Christ's Crown of Thorns. Pain and sorrow are exquisitely evoked by the drop of blood from a thorn prick on his forehead that becomes a tear running down his cheek. That tattoo's narrative *vita* counterpart is May Mann's *Elvis, Why Won't They Leave You Alone?*, in which we learn Elvis's last thoughts as he lay dying on the floor of his bathroom: "this must be like what Jesus suffered." Howard Finster (d. 2001), the famous folk artist from Georgia, created an abundance of Elvis iconography that was often inspired by photographs

of Elvis—and, he claimed, by encounters with his ghost. He did several variants on *Baby Elvis* (fig. 18), all inspired by the now-famous snapshot of the tiny Elvis, with floppy hat, held up between Gladys and Vernon; Finster's addition of wings gives the King-to-be not only an attribute of the supernatural, but also a celestial destination. In the hands of Howard Finster, a photograph, transmuted, becomes iconography. Much

FIG. 18

FIG. 19

the same iconographic outcome can be achieved simply by pairing an otherwise mundane Elvis photograph with a provocative statement about Elvis. This happened on the front page of the *Globe* of January 9, 1990, when an ordinary picture of Elvis raising his arms in triumph after finishing a song is given religious meaning by being coupled with the headline "Saint Elvis?" The King is no longer in concert; the saint is now addressing his flock.

We have seen that the *icon* of a saint is his accepted physical appearance, compositionally and stylistically crafted to achieve eye contact and spiritual dialogue with the viewer, and that the *iconography* of a saint comprises the created, evolving visual narratives giving expression to the saint's *vita*. Finally, there is *iconology* ("image study"), which is the deeper interpretation of the meaning of icons and iconography in the context in which they are set and used. The winged *Baby Elvis* by Howard Finster and the Crow of Thorns Elvis tattoo are, like the Harvey Milk icon and most icons of Saint Simeon the Stylite, iconographic concoctions with pretty simple iconology: Elvis is a celestial creature destined for heaven and Elvis suffered like Jesus. *Baby Elvis* was created for the art trade and thus not for a prescribed setting. Now it is in the collection of the High Museum in Atlanta, which means that the museum has endorsed Howard Finster as a collectible artist and Elvis as an acceptable subject. The tattoo is different insofar as its setting was from the beginning meaningful: on a fan's bicep it is a powerful and personal affirmation of the (to some) controversial assertion connecting Elvis with Jesus and martyrdom; it is fully and eternally owned and broadcast by the person who bears it.

A more complex Elvis iconographic creation with deeper and more subtle meaning was part of the window decorating contest at the Days Inn Motel during Elvis Week 1989 (fig. 19). The choice of aluminum foil for the composition's background recalls Elvis's preference for such window covering and the resulting total exclusion of daylight during the '70s. Clearly, the creator of this window understood and sympathized with Elvis in his need for darkness and seclusion as he struggled with insomnia and his health, all the while trying to gain strength so that he could go back on stage. The logo bottle cap in which Elvis's name appears is that of Pepsi Cola, his favorite soft drink; one's very recognition of this fact, unaided, would be both a satisfying demonstration of EP trivia knowledge and, for the Elvis Week pilgrims gathered there at the motel, a subtle affirmation of group affiliation or *communitas*. As for the words "ELVIS; The CHOICE OF A NEW GENERATION...," here the iconological meaning becomes more complex. This was not simply a naïve appropriation of a current jingle used to sell Pepsi, it was an affirmation by the creator of this window that devotion to Elvis was now passing to a new generation of Elvis Week pilgrims, some of whom were too young to have experienced Elvis during their lifetimes. The computer printer typeface is itself a generational statement.

FIG. 20

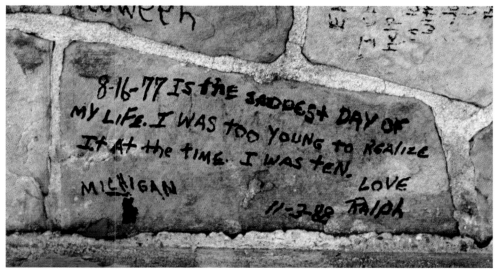

A similar spirit of generational transfer of Elvis fever was explicit in the (chronologically illogical) votive inscription on the Fans' Memorial Wall left the previous fall by a 22-year-old Graceland pilgrim named Ralph (fig. 20):

8-16-77 Is the saddest day of

my life. I was too young to realize

it at the time. I was ten.

Love

Ralph

But why the need for this Days Inn iconographic affirmation, seen mostly by fellow Elvis devotees, that young people are now choosing to affiliate themselves with things seriously Elvis? Conversation at poolside two floors below returned again and again that year to the shared hope among the originals of the Presley generation that their Elvis legacy would prosper among younger generations—a hope that by all appearances, 20 years later, is being fully realized.

A fan's votive in the Meditation Garden during that same Elvis Week in 1989 similarly derived its deeper iconographic meaning from its location and from the shared knowledge and beliefs of those who would see it there. The votive coupled

FIG. 21

yet another photograph of Elvis completing a song, this time characteristically bowing his head, with the opening words of C. Austin Miles's famous 1912 hymn *In the Garden,* that Elvis loved and recorded (fig. 21). The photo is at the center of a triptych, featuring two flanking shots of the Elvis grave intertwined with pink plastic roses. In front of the composition is a handwritten banner with the words "I come to the Garden…Alone." The words of the hymn are critical to the deeper, contextual meaning of this votive:

FIG. 22

> *I come to the garden alone*
> *While the dew is still on the roses*
> *And the voice I hear falling on my ear*
> *The Son of God discloses*

> *And He walks with me*
> *And He talks with me*
> *And He tells me I am his own*
> *And the joy we share as we tarry there*
> *None other has ever known*

The effect is to couple Elvis with Jesus and the Meditation Garden with the Garden of Gethsemane, and to insinuate the creator and the viewers of this votive into a dynamic spiritual mélange during the morning Walk Up—that very special, very private time just after sunrise when the most devoted among the fans literally come to the garden alone, and there meet and walk with both Elvis and Jesus. Clearly, this votive, like the Days Inn window, drew its meaning from being in a specific location at a specific time. Moreover, it asked something of its viewers in the completion of its meaning; in this case, they needed to know that Elvis loved and recorded this hymn, that he was profoundly religious, and that he often came to this very location during his lifetime to meditate, certainly centering his attention on Jesus. For the crowd of mid-August, all this would have been obvious—yet at the same time very meaningful.

There is a much higher level of iconographic complexity and iconological nuance to another Elvis window, this one painted on the inside of a storefront window on Beale Street; it is signed and dated "Tim 1986" (fig. 22). The picture shows Elvis on a motorcycle with flaming wheels; he is riding toward the viewer and ascending slightly. He has an enormous pair of white wings sprouting from his shoulders, and over his head, theatrically set against drawn red curtains, is an elaborate crown above a five-pointed gold star. Elvis is dressed in a tight-fitting blue suit jacket with white shirt, beige vest, red bowtie, green pants, and high boots; his hair is blue/black with a self-conscious curl drawn down over his right brow; his eyes are closed and his lips curled into his signature smile. With his left hand Elvis supports a red electric guitar on his left knee (matching that from his *'68 Comeback Special*); by contrast, his right hand points earthward, with a rivulet of butterscotch colored paint seeming to flow from his extended right index finger.

Some of the iconographic elements of Tim's composition are easily deciphered. Elvis admired and rode motorcycles—Harley-Davidsons in particular—for most of his adult life, and the poster from his 1964 movie *Roustabout* shows him riding one, though in an iconographic configuration quite different from that of the Beale Street window. The guitar, too, is a logical attribute for Elvis, though a non-electric version would have been a more typical choice; the crown overhead is fully

FIG. 23

appropriate to his status as the King, as is the heavenly reward of a gold star. The wings, the ascending path of the motorcycle, and the flaming wheels all suggest that Elvis is in some supernatural realm, headed toward Heaven, where he will receive his heavenly crown. All of these elements resonate with ancient iconography of the sun god Apollo riding his (sometimes) fiery chariot across the sky, but it is much closer to a familiar Russian iconic image of the Prophet Elijah ascending toward Heaven in his fiery chariot, in his case, led onward and upward by a winged angel; like Elvis, Elijah is passing something downward as he ascends—his sacred cloak to his disciple Elisha.

Could Tim have known this or similar Russian icons? Perhaps, but there are clues to the meaning of this picture to be found much closer at hand, in the lexicon of familiar Elvis iconography. Even those with only a passing interest in and knowledge of Elvis know that his motto TCB—"Taking Care of Business (in a Flash)"—is given graphic expression in a lightening bolt. Could the rivulet of light brown paint emanating from Elvis's right index finger be a bolt of lightening? Many among the legions of Elvis *cognoscenti* believe that his association with lightening was taken over into Presley iconography from the iconography of *Captain Marvel Comics*, which would have been familiar to anyone who, like Elvis, grew up in the '40s and '50s. In these comics, lightning is often associated with the utterance of the magical word "Shazam" and the transformation of the character from an ordinary human being into a superhero (fig. 23). These same savvy Elvis fans would also likely share in the belief that Elvis was particularly fond of Captain Marvel's son, Captain Marvel Jr. (a.k.a. "Freddy" Freeman), who was introduced into the Marvel Family pantheon via *Fawcett Comics* in 1941. (In the Elvis Presley Museum at the birth shrine in Tupelo is a window display with the young Elvis's preferred reading matter: *Captain Marvel Jr. Comics*.) Not only is it believed that Elvis collected Captain Marvel Jr. comicbooks, nearly everyone knows that he once said, upon being named among ten honorees receiving the Jaycees 1970 Outstanding Men of America Award, that as a child he imagined himself to be the hero in every comic book he read. Many believe that Elvis consciously modeled his hair style on that of Captain Marvel Jr. and that this fictional character was also the source of his peculiar preference for wearing half-length capes with high collars.

Whether Elvis Presley actually thought about Captain Marvel Jr. in this way and modeled himself on this character makes no difference in relationship to this painting, because clearly, the painter Tim believed it, and he must have thought that his viewers on Beale Street would believe it as well. And that they would share an awareness of the then-current Ghost Rider character in *Marvel Comics*, who rides a motorcycle with flaming wheels across the sky, directing his superpowers toward earth in the form of a flaming chain. The choice of colors and the graphic simplicity of the face all draw on and speak through the stylistic vocabulary of comic-book art and, specifically, *Marvel Comics*. Tim's Elvis is a hybrid of all of these, but perhaps with a message and deeper meaning all its own. As Elvis is ascending into the realm of angels, he continues to insinuate himself as a force for good into the affairs of humankind back here on earth through his (now) miraculous manipulation of lightning. This means that he still has a mission to do good things for us all—like curing that schoolteacher in Lyon of cancer with, as she testified, a bolt of lightning. This may even explain Elvis's odd outfit, with its bowtie, tight jacket, and high boots, which together may have been intended to evoke the clothing of an old-fashioned circuit riding preacher (and reference Elvis's outfit on the cover of his Gospel albums). Following this interpretation, the guitar would be taking the place of the preacher's Bible, indicating that Elvis's music is the vehicle for spreading his postmortem evangelism on the earth.

II.
GRACELAND *as LOCUS SANCTUS*

S ection I offered a definition of "saint"—informed by early Christian and contemporary Orthodox practice, and nuanced by Max Weber's notion of charisma—in which Elvis Presley, among others, can comfortably fit as a "secular charismatic martyr." Once so positioned, Elvis's saint-like characteristics (miracles, relics, icons, *vitae,* and such) were explored in depth, leading to the inevitable though unstated conclusion that while other such secular charismatic martyrs—Harvey Milk, Selena, Michael Jackson, *et cetera*—certainly have many of those same characteristics, including attributed miracles, none among them manifests that aggregation of saint-like characteristic on the level of Elvis Presley.

Section II will follow a similar trajectory by offing a definition of *locus sanctus,* or "holy site," that is broader and more nuanced than generally understood in strictly religious terms, with the two-fold aim of positioning Graceland as a secular *locus sanctus* (for a charismatic martyr) and then positioning it within that subcategory of holy site as the preeminent exemplar. The narrative will begin with the very specific concept of *locus sanctus* as understood in early Christianity, as exemplified by the Church of the Holy Sepulchure in Jerusalem and shrine of Saint Simeon Stylites at Qal`at Sem`ān in northern Syria. It will then bring that concept forward into the post-medieval Christian world and the western hemisphere, and then broaden it significantly beyond its religious boundaries to include, first, pilgrimage destinations associated with "victims of unjust death," and second, those associated with secular charismatic martyrs like Elvis.

The Holy Sepulchre *and* Qal`at Sem`ān

The saint has his *locus sanctus* or "holy place." This is how we know him for who he is and how we know where to find him, and this, in part, is how he has traditionally manifested his miraculous powers on earth. Holy places—which, like the saints that make them holy, are to be found in many cultures and religions—have been an especially prominent part of Christianity since the 4th century. For the faithful, their physical attraction was and remains intense: a holy place presupposes pilgrimage and pilgrimage requires a holy place. A *locus sanctus* could be the location of an important relic, like the chair in which the Virgin sat during the Annunciation, or the site of miraculous waters, like the leper-curing Baths of Elijah. Or in its more familiar form, it could be the setting of some major event in the life of Christ, like the Nativity or the Crucifixion. But outside the Holy Land, where the Old and New Testaments have dominated the sacred landscape of Christianity for nearly two millennia, a *locus sanctus* usually turns out to be the home of a saint. It might be the place of a saint still living (a holy man) or, more likely, the place of his bodily remains, sealed in a tomb or reliquary and enshrined in elaborate architecture: the martyr ("witness") for Christ enshrined in his *martyrion*. Besides bodily remains and a shrine, a *locus sanctus* will typically have related contact relics; moreover, it will often be a place of miraculous healings and it will certainly be a destination for pilgrimage, whose timing is usually linked to the anniversaries of the shrine's sanctifying events.

Christians have believed for many centuries that the sacred power of a saintly body or a miraculous event literally charges its physical surroundings with holiness and that to be there on that spot is to partake in that holiness (again, Frazer's "law of contact"). But what is now taken for granted by hundreds of millions of Christians worldwide was not always part of Christian belief. Initially, the Holy Land was simply Palestine and Jerusalem, then called *Aelia Capitolina*, and was only one among many locations in Palestine that bore witness to the historical truth of Jesus the man—as Athens was and is for Plato. Emperor Constantine's act of unearthing and enshrining the Tomb of Christ in the early 4th century marked a critical transformation in attitude, after which the documentary dimension of Jerusalem and Palestine, and of important Christian sites and objects generally, was superseded by their spiritual dimension—by the belief that they bore sacred power and thus miracle-working potential. Moreover, what applied to early Christian Palestine on the level of its typography applied on a much smaller scale to virtually any object that had come in contact with the sacred. The theologian John of

Damascus (d. 749) explained the sanctity, and thus the attraction of the True Cross, in terms of sacred contact: the cross is to be adored "because it has been sanctified by contact with the sacred body and blood." Similarly, while discussing earth taken out from the Tomb of Christ and its ability to cure diseases and repel snakes, Gregory, bishop of Tours (d. 594/5) observed that "faith believes that everything the sacred body touches is holy."

Jerusalem's Church of the Holy Sepulchre, the architectural ensemble enshrining the rock-cut Tomb of Christ, is Christianity's most important *locus sanctus*. A vast complex of courtyards and colonnades, destroyed and rebuilt several times, it was conceived and constructed in the early 4th century by Emperor Constantine. Within its footprint are Golgotha, the site of the Crucifixion, and the Holy Sepulchre, the place of Christ's entombment after his body was taken down from the cross. Three centuries after the historical event that sanctified this spot, Christ's Tomb was miraculously "discovered" by Saint Helen, Constantine's mother, on her son's behalf, in excavations beneath a pagan temple. The most important relics in

FIG. 24

the Church of the Holy Sepulchre, which she then built to replace the temple, are the Tomb itself, sculpted out of the living rock of a hillside and once richly embellished with gold and silver (fig. 24), the nearby hillock of Golgotha, with its own chapel enshrining the crevice in the rock where the cross of the Crucifixion was set, and the True Cross, initially kept close by in its own chapel; at one point, its sacred treasures included the Holy Grail, described by the Piacenza pilgrim as an onyx cup. Constantine and Helen also built churches to enshrine the two other main *loca sancta* of the Holy Land: the Nativity Cave in Bethlehem and the Ascension Mount just east of Jerusalem. Constantine was responsible as well for erecting another of Christianity's great *martyria*, Saint Peter's Basilica in Rome, which to this day—though now in the form of Michelangelo's famous 16th-century renovation— enshrines the bones of the Apostle Peter, who the faithful believe was crucified upside down at that spot in AD 64.

Like the 4th century, the 12th and 13th centuries—the age of the great Gothic cathedrals—was a time when magnificent church architecture arose in response to saintly remains to create *loca sancta* that remain famous to this day. Chartres Cathedral near Paris was built to enshrine the Veil of the Virgin Mary, Reims Cathedral in the Champagne region of northeast France was built to enshrine part of the skull of John the Baptist, and Sainte Chapelle, the exquisite little chapel on the Ile de la Cité in the center of Paris, was created as a grand architectural reliquary for the Crown of Thorns. Like the fragment of John the Baptist's skull at Reims, the Crown of Thorns had been stolen from Constantinople during the Crusader sack of the city in 1204 and carried off to France—only to be lost six centuries later during the French Revolution. There are thousands more *loca sancta* of every description and size, from those that dominate an entire city to those hidden away in a forest or isolated on a mountaintop, from those commanding international pilgrimage to those drawing pious traffic only from a nearby village. Just a fraction of the world's *loca sancta* date from the first millennium of Christianity and a smaller proportion still is to be found on the sacred real estate of Christ and the Apostles.

When Simeon the Stylite died in the late summer of 459, no architectural monument existed atop the rocky bluff where he had spent the last four decades of his life; there was only his vacant column, this holy site's counterpart relic to the

FIG. 25

Tomb of Christ and the Virgin's Veil. Within the next 30 years, however, there rose from that sacred spot a vast cross-shaped *martyrion* consisting of four churches radiating from the sides of a central octagon, within which stood Simeon's famous column, today just a fraction of its original size thanks to 15 centuries of relic collectors (fig. 25). The cruciform architectural complex surrounding Simeon's column is nearly equal in floor space to Byzantium's most famous building, the Church of Hagia Sophia, which was constructed about 40 years later in Constantinople. Yet unlike Hagia Sophia, Simeon's *martyrion* was set on a barren hill 40 miles from the nearest city; moreover, it was part of a huge, walled complex that included a monastery, two smaller churches, several large hostels, and a campground for Simeon pilgrims. Presumably it was Emperor Zeno (d. 491) who funded this huge project and brought together to this remote site the architect, sculptors, and masons needed to realize it. No one knows for sure, though one thing is certain: such a compound in such a remote place presupposes enormous pilgrim traffic. And what makes this site, Qal`at Sem`ān, so impressive is that the entire project was completed in just a few decades, and only after Simeon had died and his body had been carried away to Antioch. Its draw for pilgrims was the column itself and the earth from the hill upon which it stood, which they believed had been sanctified by contact with the column.

Preeminent *loca sancta*, including the Holy Sepulchre and the shrine of Saint Simeon Stylites, were replicated in various forms, and through their replication carried the spiritual potency of the model to distant locations. For Simeon, the copy was realized full scale just once, in the form of another stylite who took the name of Simeon, practicing his asceticism a century and a half after Simeon "the elder" on a column near Antioch. By contrast, copies of the Holy Sepulchre exist in a multiplicity of version all over the world. The Tomb was often copied all by itself, typically functioning as a baptistery, since there was (and is) believed to be a symbolic connection between the Resurrection of Christ and the "resurrection" of the faithful into eternal life through baptism. Among the most beautiful such architectural offspring of Chirst's Tomb is the ornate baptistery in front of the cathedral in Pisa. Occasionally, the entire sacred topography of Jerusalem, including the Tomb, was replicated. Certainly the most spectacular "transplanted" Jerusalem is that built by Emperor Gebre Mesqel Lalibela around 1200 in a small town in northern Ethiopia that now bears his name (Lalibela); amazingly, the dozen churches in the complex are monoliths, built down into the living rock of the site.

"Modern" *Loca Sancta*

Post-medieval *loca sancta* differ from the holy sites of earlier times insofar as they are not to be found in the sacred territory of the Old Testament or of Christ, or even of the early Christian saints, but rather, they are mostly located in parts of the world where Christianity was a much later arrival. Their sanctifying event, therefore, typically has a different flavor from those of early *loca sancta*, since it cannot be linked to the earthly activities of a biblical figure, but rather depends on a much more recent holy person or miraculous apparition. In the case of two of the four holy sites discussed in this section, the Virgin Mary made the location sacred by miraculously appearing there to a naïve but worthy believer; in 1531 she appeared in Mexico City as Our Lady of Guadalupe, leaving behind her miracle-working image, and in 1858 she appeared in a small town in southwestern France as Our Lady of Lourdes, leaving behind the healing waters of her sacred Grotto.

Our Lady of Guadalupe

According to official Catholic accounts, Juan Diego, an Aztec commoner of about 55, while walking from his home village to Mexico City in the early morning of December 9, 1531, saw a vision of a teen-age girl surrounded by light on the slopes of the Hill of Tepeyac. The girl asked him to build a temple on the site in her honor.

Juan Diego recognized the apparition to be that of the Virgin Mary and went to tell his story to the Spanish bishop, who responded with skepticism. Juan Diego then retuned to the hill, and this time the "Lady of Heaven" was waiting for him and insisted that he pursue the bishop, who, on his second encounter with the peasant, showed more interest, asking that he secure a sign from the Lady. When the Lady of Heaven heard this, she instructed Juan Diego to gather flowers from the top of the hill even though it was winter and no flowers were then blooming. To his surprise, he found and gathered fragrant Castilian roses, which the Lady herself rearranged on his outstretched *tilma* (peasant cloak). Juan Diego went straight to the bishop and, after telling him the entire story, opened his cloak, and as the flowers fell to the floor:

> *...there suddenly appeared [on the tilma] the precious image of the ever-Virgin St. Mary, Mother of God, just exactly as it is even now in her temple of Tepeyac, in her church which is named Guadalupe.*

Today a 16th-century church stands on that site, and since it is relatively small and sinking into the dehydrated topsoil of Mexico City, Juan Diego's *tilma* with its miraculous image of the Virgin is displayed instead in the adjacent modern shrine, where it can be venerated as one passes it on a walkalator (fig. 26)—which

FIG. 26

FIG. 27

for some pilgrims, ironically, follows a slow and painful approach to the shrine on their knees. Nearby is the very spot of Juan Diego's apparition of December 1531, now complemented in a special chapel with a statue of the saint, to which are affixed vast numbers of tiny votives (*Milagros*) attesting to his power. Testifying to the power of the miraculous image of Our Lady of Guadalupe is a grotesquely bent crucifix in a display window in the new shrine, which once deflected the force of an anarchist's bomb and saved Juan Diego's sacred *tilma*. The shops leading up to the shrine are filled not only with the stuff of the pilgrims' physical nourishment but also with the stuff of their spiritual nourishment, tailored to suit the needs of Mexican Catholics, including the "Child Doctor Jesus" (*Niño Doctor Jesus*) with white coat and stethoscope (fig. 27), playing his part as the national agent of miraculous healing.

In the case of Our Lady of Guadalupe, the bearer of sacred power is not some base substance like dirt or oil that has had contact with an important relic; rather, it is the image of the relic itself, whose millions of copies distributed throughout the world spread, as if by some sacred pandemic, the potential for miracles which resides in the original in Mexico City. In some instances, the entire ensemble of Juan Diego's miraculous apparition is reconstituted in a distant location as a tableau vivant and there receives its own prayers and votives (fig. 28). The miraculous appearance of Our Lady of Guadalupe to someone in distress is both a sign of and a vehicle for salvation. A votive to one of Our Lady's salvation miracles shows a prisoner in the notorious prison at Celaya, Mexico, about to escape a firing squad, thanks to her intervention through her image, which appears miraculously above the prison's open gate (fig. 29):

*This Milagro [votive] is
dedicated to the Most Saintly
Virgin of Guadalupe February
11, 1933
Pedro Morales Celaya, GTO*

Relics and icons are close cousins. The Ascension Mount, with the footprints of Jesus, and the Column of the Flagellation, with the handprints of Jesus, were both relics, much like the wood of the True Cross. But unlike the True Cross, they bore imprints of Jesus's body—the beginnings of icons. The inevitable next step was for Jesus to leave iconic contact images of his face and his whole body. Orthodox Christians call such relic/icons *acheiropoietiai*, which in Greek means "(images) not made by human hands." The

FIG. 28

Shroud of Turin with its full-body imprint of Christ, from the mid-14th century, and Juan Diego's *tilma*, from the early 16th century, are Christianity's two most famous surviving *acheiropoietiai*. One of the earliest of these miraculous imprint icons, now lost, was preserved in Memphis, Egypt, and seen there around 570 by the pilgrim from Piacenza:

> We saw there a piece of linen on which is a portrait of the Savior. People
> say he once wiped his face with it, and that the outline remained. It is
> venerated at various times and we also venerated it, but it was too bright
> for us to concentrate on since, as you went on concentrating, it changed
> before your eyes.

Around the same time, the textile *acheiropoietos* of Christ's face that was eventually to save Constantinople from the Avars turned up at the bottom of a woman's well in Asia Minor—though this renowned object, too, has long since vanished. In

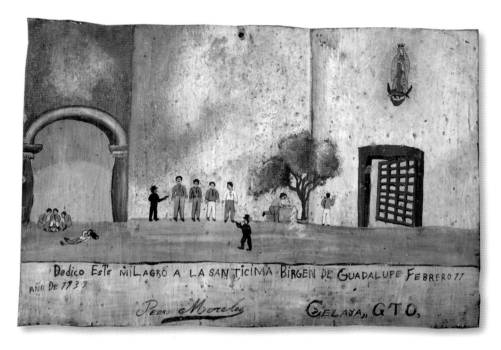

Dedico Este miLagró A LA SANTiciMA BiRGEN DE GUADALUPE FeBRERO 77 AÑO DE 1933

Pedro Morales

GELAYA„ GTO.

FIG. 29

628, the Avars, from the territory of modern Bulgaria, laid siege to the Byzantine capital; at the point when the city's walls and military defenders seemed incapable of saving the city and empire, this miraculous cloth icon of Christ was brought to the walls and the Avars were repelled. Over the centuries this famous relic/icon, and many less famous man-made icons with similar miraculous credentials, performed thousands of miracles, which often involved repelling the impious acts of individual non-believers or the attacks of entire infidel armies. In the 12th century, an icon of the Virgin and Child in the Cathedral of Saint Sophia in Novgorod, in northern Russia, miraculously repelled the arrows of the attackers from nearby Suzdal. Such traditions die hard, even in the face of repression. During the Russian constitutional crisis of October 1993 and the Communist siege of the Parliament building, supporters of Boris Yeltsin took their personal icons to display at the ramparts—thereby, in their view, achieving a similar miraculous outcome to the one in Novgorod eight centuries earlier.

El Sanctuario de Chimayo

In the desert hills 24 miles north of Santa Fe is one of Christianity's newer sacred places: *El Sanctuario de Chimayo* (fig. 30). Unassuming by medieval standards, its shrine is a simple adobe sanctuary, its "witness" a kettle-size hole in the clay floor of a side chapel (fig. 31). According to an often-repeated legend, Chimayo is a *locus sanctus*—most notably for New Mexico's Hispanic Catholics—because on the night of Good Friday in 1813, a Chimayo friar performing his penance saw a light radiating from a hillside near the Santa Cruz River. He dug a hole at the source of that light and discovered a miraculous crucifix, which was soon named Our Lord of Esquipulas. When the local priest in Santa Cruz heard of this wonderful crucifix, he and a group set out for Chimayo and in solemn procession took the sacred object back to his church in Santa Cruz, placing it on the altar and closing the building for the night. The next morning, to everyone's amazement, Our Lord of Esquipulas was gone from the church and back in its sacred hole in Chimayo. A second procession to Santa Cruz was organized and the crucifix returned to the altar, but again, and for a third time, it miraculously returned to that hole in the hillside near the Santa Cruz

FIG. 30

FIG. 31

River. By then everyone understood that *El Señor de Esquipulas* wanted to remain in Chimayo, so a small chapel was built on the site. Miracles followed, and in 1816 that chapel was enlarged into the present sanctuary.

It is to *El Posito*, the "sacred pit," that the lame and blind come to this day seeking cures. Many use the soil to make a muddy mixture that if eaten or applied to the skin is believed to have miraculous healing powers. The adjacent Vigil Store once housed an unusual number of soda machines, which the owner said were needed by pilgrims who ingested the holy dirt on site and started choking. For the majority of the faithful who choose instead to take their portion of *tierra bendita* ("blessed earth") away with them, the Vigil Store stocks a wide variety of small containers with appropriate Chimayo iconography. The elegance with which the ever-so-discrete "sand lady" replenishes the miraculous sand in the sacred pit with the mundane sand from along the nearby Santa Cruz River behind the church is a minor miracle in and of itself, though when pilgrim traffic is especially intense, as on Good Friday, there are hundreds of pre-packed plastic bags of *tierra bendita* laid out on the altar ready for the taking.

Not only is the original crucifix, Our Lord of Esquipulas, still in place over the altar, there is a second powerful religious work of art nearby. Called *El Niño de Atocha* ("The Holy Child of Atocha"), it is in a side chapel next to the small room with the sacred sand. *El Niño* is believed to wander about freely at night when the shrine is closed, doing all sorts of good works, and so the faithful offer him baby shoes to replace the tiny footwear that he consumes on his nightly excursions (fig. 32). Because this little figure of Jesus is so amazingly ambulatory, Chimayo and

its sacred dirt are believed especially
powerful for healing those who have
difficulty walking. This accounts for the
many crutches and prosthetic limbs
that are left behind (fig. 33) and for
the votive thanks for such healings on
the walls near the sacred hole with its
sanctified soil.

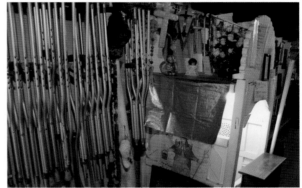

We have already encountered
miracle-working dirt at the shrine of
Saint Simeon, where typically, such
dirt was made portable for pilgrims
in the form of small disks, impressed
with an image of Simeon doing his
good works from the top of his column
(fig. 34). The classic holy dirt *locus
sanctus* of the early Christian period,
though, is associated with Jesus him-

FIG. 32
FIG. 33

self. Sulpicius Severus, writing in the early 5th century, described a famous sacred
spot in the sand on top of the Ascension Mount where "are still to be seen" the
footprints of Jesus, despite the fact that pilgrims "compete with one another" to
carry the sand away. (Clearly, the Ascension Mount then had its own version of the
"sand lady.") Nowadays packets of sacred dirt from a variety of sanctifying sources
are available for purchase all over Jerusalem and Israel more generally, as are little
boxes with tiny chips of holy rock from, for example, the House of Saints Peter and
Andrew in Capharnaum.

An early pilgrim's box for sacred souvenirs in the Vatican suggests what it
might have been like to make the collecting rounds of holy sites 1,400 years ago
(fig. 35). The box is filled with bits of earth, wood, and cloth embedded in resin
that together constitute a pilgrim's personal collection of sacred souvenirs; some
still have readable labels, such as "from the Mount of Olives" or "from Sion."
The underside of the lid is painted with five scenes from the life of Christ—the

FIG. 34

Nativity, Baptism, Crucifixion, Women at the Tomb, and Ascension—each of which is associated with a stop along the Holy Land pilgrimage route. The connection between picture and souvenir at first seems only generic, since there are labeled rocks in the box (e.g., that "from Sion") that have no corresponding image. Yet there is a more subtle layer of meaning, since there are aspects of the pictures that match what the pilgrim would actually have seen at the sacred site but do not match what the Bible says happened there. The clearest example is the picture at the upper left of the Women at the Tomb of Jesus (Matthew 28:1-8, etc.), which shows instead of the cave-tomb described in the Gospels the small tomb structure that Emperor Constantine had built out of the remains of that cave in the early 4th century.

The substitution was made because in the eyes of the pilgrim, the Tomb of Christ was not simply a piece of architecture, it was a large contact relic—in fact, Christianity's most important contact relic. For the pilgrim, a picture of the Tomb was spiritually powerful all by itself, much as the Tomb as a physical thing was

FIG. 35

powerful. (The same relationship exists between images of Our Lady of Guadalupe and Juan Diego's sacred *tilma*.) The Piacenza pilgrim described how he entered Jerusalem and venerated the Tomb of Christ, just as, a few minutes later, he was to venerate the Wood of the Cross, which was kept nearby; both, for him, were relics and both could re-transfer their sacred power. He later notes that "earth is brought to the Tomb and put inside, and those who go in take some as a blessing." The owner of the Vatican relic box was probably among them, since one of his collectibles is labeled "from the Life-Giving [Tomb of Christ]."

Our Lady of Lourdes

On February 11, 1858, on the outskirts of the tiny French market town of Lourdes, nestled in the foothills of the Pyrenees, a 14-year-old girl named Bernadette Soubirous saw an apparition of a beautiful woman in the remote Grotto of Massabielle; this was the first of 18 similar apparitions she alone was to witness at that location, the last of which took place on July 16 that summer. In a later appearance to Bernadette, the beautiful woman identified herself as the "Immaculate Conception," which the faithful took to be the Blessed Virgin Mary. With each successive apparition, a greater number of local believers accompanied Bernadette Soubirous, though none among them ever saw what she saw. Nor did they hear from the beautiful woman, as Bernadette heard, the instruction to kiss the ground, to light candles, to drink of the water of the sacred Grotto, and to bathe there. Over the course of these apparitions, two healing miracles took place at the Grotto of Massabielle, one of which involved Bernadette herself; the girl's votive candle burned down to her flesh, but her flesh was not burned. The second miracle involved Bernadette's friend Catherine Latapie. During the night of the 12th apparition, on March 1, she plunged her dislocated arm into the waters of the Grotto's spring and regained free movement. Within a year, thousands of pilgrims were visiting the Grotto, and in 1864 a statue of Our Lady of Lourdes was erected there.

Much as the miraculous apparition of Our Lady of Guadalupe to Juan Diego is replicated in regional shrines worldwide, so also is the apparition of Our Lady of Lourdes to Bernadette Sourbirous reconstituted far and wide, even in the back yards of suburban American homes; each local shrine is a place for prayers and votives, and, presumably, the potential agent of the miraculous. Lourdes pilgrims take home

with them a medallion or a bottle attesting to their visit (fig. 36) and gallons of healing water from the Grotto, useful against all sort of maladies for years to come (fig. 37).

Since the mid-19th century, more than 200 million pilgrims have made their way to Lourdes, mostly during its summer season, from the beginning of April to the end of October; yearly visitation is currently estimated at 3.5 million. Despite the town's small size (just 15,000 inhabitants), Lourdes and its environs have more hotels than any French destination other than Paris. Nowadays, the Lourdes website provides a live cam feed 24/7 with worldwide visual and audio access to the sacred Grotto, as well as email contacts for those who cannot make the pilgrimage in person so that on-site volunteers might, on their behalf, place their specific prayers and votives at the Grotto; moreover, these armchair pilgrims can order online their own portion of sanctified Lourdes water to be delivered by mail.

Each day large numbers of pilgrims in wheelchairs partake in a ritualized

FIG. 37

encounter with the Grotto. At set times, these infirm emerge from hospices and hospitals lining the route leading down toward the sacred spring, one attendant pushing the wheelchair from behind and the other pulling (fig. 38). The infirm are organized into two tight columns, each following a parallel path articulated in red along the roadway.

Access to the Grotto for the general public is interrupted for an extended period as these parallel rows of sick pilgrims, some clearly near death, are brought into the Grotto; typically, they touch its stone wall as they get close (fig. 39), take a photograph if they are able, and are photographed by a hospice volunteer as they emerge on the far side. Some will continue on to immerse themselves in the private pools of healing water (for men and for women) that are found just beyond the row of enclosed metal stands for their votive candles. Like all visitors, those in wheelchairs, or family or volunteers acting on their behalf, will collect sacred water from the small spigots that are set in polished marble walls that sheath the rough stone of the hillside, just before the sacred spring.

Nearly 3 million Moslem pilgrims visit Mecca each year during the four days of the *Hajj* alone. And in Mecca, too, there is a stone to be touched by the faithful as part of the encounter ritual. The ritual is called *Tawaf*, and it consists of seven counter-clockwise circumambulations of the Kaaba as it stands in the vast courtyard of the Great Mosque. One million of the devote can participate at a time, so not all are able to reach the Kaaba's cornerstone, the "Black Stone," believed

to date back to the time of Adam and Eve and to have been kissed by Mohammad himself. Those lucky and determined enough to press forward to the prize will kiss and then briefly touch the stone (in fact, eight stone fragments embedded in wax), before burly security guards push them away. Like the grotto stone at Lourdes, the Black Stone at Mecca has long since acquired permanent blackness for having been touched by millions of the pious.

It may seem odd, given the enormous traffic of the infirm at Lourdes, but according to the Shrine's website, the Catholic Church has officially documented and accepted only 67 miracles at Lourdes itself. The elaborate vetting process is not unlike that used to identify Catholic saints; it includes doctors of all sorts and scientists when needed, and a two-step review, first by the on-site Medical Bureau, established in 1905 by Pope Pius X, and then, if that hurdle is passed, a second review by the International Medical Committee, established in 1947, which consists of a blue-ribbon panel of 20 specialists. Miracle #67, which was declared a true miracle on November 9, 2005, actually took place more than a half century earlier, on August 19, 1952. It involved a 41-year old Italian invalid named Anna Santaniello, who suffered from severe heart disease; Anna was brought to the Grotto on a stretcher but left under her own power and took part that evening in the Torchlight Procession—a ritual that is still the dramatic culmination of each day's sacred activities at Lourdes.

The healing power of sanctified water was a familiar sight to the pilgrim from Piacenza. He took a dip in the spring at Cana, where Jesus had miraculously transformed water into wine at a wedding, "to gain a blessing" (Greek, *eulogia*)—that is, its sacred, healing power. And later in his journey, after his climb up Mount Tabor, he crossed the Jordan to the city of Gadara, and then traveled on to the site of some pre-Christian hot springs called the Baths of Elijah, where his diary notes that: "Lepers are cleansed there, and have their meals from the inn there at public expense." As at Lourdes, the encounter of the infirm with the healing waters is ritualized:

> *The baths fill in the evening. In front of the basin is a large tank. When it is full, all the gates are closed, and they [the lepers] are sent in through a small door with lights [candles, oil lamps] and incense, and sit in the tank all night. They fall asleep, and the person who is going to be cured sees a vision. ... In one week he is cleansed.*

But certainly the most famous holy water *locus sanctus* in the world of early Christian pilgrimage was that at the River Jordan, at the spot where John the Baptist was believed to have baptized Christ; its feast day, January 6—also the Feast of the Epiphany—is still celebrated there and worldwide. When the pilgrim from Piacenza kept the Feast of the Epiphany at that famous *locus sanctus,* he saw the water of the Jordan miraculously turn back on itself "with a roar" at the moment when the priest started his blessing, and he saw the water stay there as the gathered neophytes entered the Jordan to be baptized. Once the formal baptism had been completed, everyone else assembled at the site that day went down into the water "to gain a blessing"; moreover, the Piacenza Pilgrim noted in his diary that some among them wore linen or other special garments that "will serve them as their shrouds for burial." He also noted that the ship owners of Alexandria had representatives in attendance that day, carrying "great jars of spices and balsam." As soon as the river had been blessed but before the baptism started, these men poured out the contents of the jars into the Jordan and then drew out holy water that they planned to use "for sprinkling their ships when they are about to set sail." Although no iconographic containers for sanctified Jordan water survive from the early Christian period, they are commonplace nowadays in Jerusalem, where they are often sold as part of a set, with oil that has touched the stone of the Holy Sepulchre (fig. 40).

The Oratory of Saint Joseph

Healing the lame is the long-established specialty of the Oratory of Saint Joseph, the enormous pilgrimage church that rises on Mount Royale above the city of Montreal (fig. 41). It is the legacy of André Bessette (1845-1937), a miracle-working lay brother of the Order of the Holy Cross. Like Saint Simeon, André revealed his intense spirituality as a child through extraordinary penances, which greatly alarmed his friends and loved ones. In his late 20s he took his vows, and since he had been sickly and frail from birth, he was assigned the simple duties of door-keeper at Notre Dame College on Mount Royale, a job that he kept for 40 years. Brother André was devoted to Saint Joseph, foster-father of Jesus and patron saint of Canada, travelers, houses and real estate agents, and working folks generally.

FIG. 40

In addition to being the college doorkeeper, Good Brother André was tasked with visiting sick students, and soon he gained the reputation of being the "miracle worker of Mount Royale," because of the various healings he achieved through prayers invoking Saint Joseph; typically these were accompanied by rubbing on a bit of blessed oil drawn from the lamp that burned in front of the statue of Saint Joseph in the college chapel. An early cure was documented in a French magazine of May 9, 1878; it involved the healing of Brother Alderic, bursar at Notre Dame, who asked "little" Brother André to fetch him some oil from the lamp of Saint Joseph, that he had heard so much about. That evening Brother Alderic applied a few drops from his "precious vial" on a leg wound, while praying to Saint Joseph for a cure. And sure enough, at the end of two days his wound was completely healed.

Eventually Brother André was receiving hundreds of pilgrims each day at a rate of 30 to 40 an hour. He would greet them warmly, listen to their stories, and then rub them gently with the oil of Saint Joseph; 435 cures were recorded in 1916 alone. Brother André's immediate superiors were uncomfortable both with his enormous popularity and with his hundreds of reputed cures. The diocesan authorities remained suspicious throughout his lifetime, and doctors openly called him a quack; some even labeled his oil-rubbing technique as prurient. Yet, through all of these trials, the popular recognition of Brother André's charismatic healing powers prevailed, finally taking grand architectural form in the huge Oratory of Saint Joseph, which took more than 50 years to complete. In 1940, the Archbishop of Montreal instituted the beatification process and on May 23, 1982, Brother Andé was declared "Blessed" by Pope John Paul II. But despite miracles, good works, and a magnificent shrine, advocates for André Bessette—the Good Brother André—had to wait nearly three more decades until he finally achieved sainthood, in October 2010.

In January 1937, when Brother André died at age 92, one million people filed past his coffin. Today a museum in the Oratory is devoted to his life and spirit; it includes a bank vault with a monstrance displaying André's embalmed heart— which was stolen in 1972 but recovered in 1973. It includes as well stark dioramas reconstructing Brother André's austere living and working quarters, one of which has a full-size mannequin of André performing his doorkeeper duties (fig. 42). Miracles were and still are achieved on Mount Royale by way of Saint Joseph oil,

FIG.41

FIG. 42

which is drawn from a small copper tub at the foot of a statue of Saint Joseph and the Christ Child. Vast numbers of cures, specifically of the lame, are attested to by hundreds of votive plaques and discarded wooden crutches (fig. 43); the chapel near the sacred oil is filled with a sea of votive candles that warm the air and give a sweet fragrance to the entire church.

Like the story of sacred earth, the story of sacred oil is an old one in Christianity. The diary of the Piacenza pilgrim describes an impressive ceremony for the blessing of oil in small flasks that regularly took place in the Church of the Holy Sepulchre. When the Cross is brought out of the small room for veneration "a star appears in the sky, and comes over the place where they lay the Cross." The faithful venerate the sacred relic by bowing to the ground before it and, perhaps, by kissing it, and then offer little flasks of oil to be blessed. When the mouth of one of these flasks touches the wood of the Cross, "the oil instantly bubbles over, and unless it is closed very quickly it all spills out."

About four dozen sacred oil flasks survive from the period of the Piacenza pilgrim; they are made of pewter, are slightly larger than a quarter, and they bear images on both sides, typically evoking the True and the Holy Sepulchre Cross (fig. 44). Their images of the Holy Sepulchre match that of the Vatican relic box, insofar as they show Constantine's 4th-century architecturally-embellished Tomb and not the tomb-cave described in the Gospels. Like Our Lady of Guadalupe, the transfer of sacred power is here derived at least in part by the identity of the image with a famous relic. Nowadays sanctified oil is available for purchase in little bottles all over Jerusalem. There is even a small sales stall that abuts the back of the Tomb of Christ itself, owned and

FIG. 43

operated by the Coptic Orthodox Church, whose oil is said to have touched the very rock that the body of Jesus had once touched.

Loca Sancta for Victims of Unjust Death
Roadside Shrines

Along the highways of the world are familiar *loca sancta* of a (mostly) very private and personal sort. These are the sacred spots that are created *ad hoc* by grieving relatives for their loved ones who died there in a car crash. The stories behind hundreds of them were collected in 2005 by Marcii ("Mustang Marcii") Magliulo in *Crosses Across our Nation*. In August 2004 she set out in a motor home with her dog, following the University of Nevada, Las Vegas women's soccer team for whom her daughter Annii then played. It was a journey that, as Marcii said "would change my life and the lives of so many others." As it turned out, Marcii was to cover more than 15,000 miles across 14 states and as she did, roadside memorials went from being a curiosity to being a fixation. She stopped, photographed, and left a note,

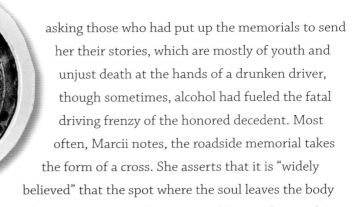

FIG. 44

asking those who had put up the memorials to send her their stories, which are mostly of youth and unjust death at the hands of a drunken driver, though sometimes, alcohol had fueled the fatal driving frenzy of the honored decedent. Most often, Marcii notes, the roadside memorial takes the form of a cross. She asserts that it is "widely believed" that the spot where the soul leaves the body is somehow important to the success of that soul in reaching heaven. The book is organized by state, and the submitted stories, which usually occupy a single page, are accompanied by a photo of the memorial and of the victim. After these narratives, Marcii provides tips on how to help change state laws involving drunk drivers and then she lists the various memorial funds set up for the victims, with contact information.

What Marcii did not include, though she might have, are those roadside *loca sancta* associated with famous or near-famous people, like the James Dean Memorial Junction at the intersection of routes #41 and #46 in southern California, and Pre's Rock on Skyline Boulevard just east of the University of Oregon in Eugene. The truculent *Rebel Without a Cause* actor died at his junction on September 30, 1955, at age 24, in his Porsche, after a head-on-collision that apparently was not his fault, whereas the equally truculent 24-year-old long distance runner Steve Prefrontaine died at his rock on May 30, 1975, after flipping his MGB while drunk. The memorial for Prefontaine was dedicated in 1997 and is maintained by Eugene Parks and Recreation; it regularly receives track pilgrims who typically leave an item of their running paraphernalia. James Dean's memorial, near the tiny town of Cholame, was the point of convergence for several hundred Dean fans and a few look-alikes on the 50th anniversary of his death in 2005.

Roadside crosses are especially popular in the southwest among Hispanic Americans, who call them *descansos* or "resting places," recalling the Spanish tradition of marking those locations between church and cemetery where processing pallbearers stopped to put the coffin down and rest. Perhaps this regional popularity is only to be expected, especially in New Mexico, where there is an unusual problem with drinking and driving and an extraordinary fondness for ornate cemetery memorials, typically accompanied by an abundance of bright plastic flowers. North of Santa Fe, in the eight miles leading westward on route #76 toward Española, there are 11 roadside memorials easily recognized at 50 miles an hour; certainly there are more of the understated sort.

The most elaborate among them comprises a large lacquered wooden cross with a surrounding *locus sanctus* embellished with artificial flowers and demarcated by a metal fence; lights are positioned within the fence to illuminate the cross for nighttime viewing (fig. 45):

BORN
7-6-70
IN LOVING MEMORY OF
TOMMY E MARTINEZ
ESTAS CON DIOS
DIED
1-2-98
FAMILY
CORAL SAMANTHA STEVEN

FIG. 45

FIG. 46

At the top of the cross is a white scroll with the letters *I N R I*. This abbreviation commonly appears on crucifixes from the earliest centuries of Christian art; it refers to an identifying plaque put up by the Roman soldiers and stands for the Latin *Iesus Nazaranzenus Rex Iudiorum,* "Jesus of Nazareth, King of the Jews." This memorial, when it was photographed in July 2009, was just a few feet from a tree whose bark had then recently been stripped by the impact of a careening car, part of which (a shattered rearview mirror) lay nearby. Certainly there was a connection, but not a recent one, since the decedent Tommy Martinez died more than a decade earlier in an accident at this same site.

The urban variant on these typically rural memorials are those put up, often by groups of friends as opposed to family, for victims of murder. At about 11 pm on a Sunday evening in late July 2010, Stephen Pitcairn, a Johns Hopkins University lab assistant, was confronted on his way home from Penn Train Station in Baltimore, by a young addict and his girlfriend. Stabbed in the chest, he died on the edge of the street in the arms of a nearby resident, still on his cell phone with his mother in Florida. Three days later, on what would have been Stephen's 24th birthday, friends celebrated at a makeshift memorial assembled at the tree closest to the spot of his death (fig. 46). In addition to the several photographs of the smiling young researcher affixed with red ribbon to the tree, there was at its base a chocolate cake, red licorice whips, and three oysters on the half-shell; a bouquet of red roses lay at the left and carnations at the right. Within days Baltimore City employees had cleared the site, though it continued to be replenished by Stephen's friends months later.

To those charged with clearing snow, mowing grass or cleaning the sidewalk, these spiritually embellished bits of the edge of highway or street are a nuisance, and to the rest of us they may have little or no meaning at all, but for those who have lost someone in an accident or by murder, they have been raised to the level of personal *loca sancta*. They are worthy of a marker for all passersby to see and that marker is worthy of careful, respectful maintenance—and visits, often, but certainly on the anniversary of the tragic event. Think now not of a single family and a small circle of friends but of Elvis and Graceland and of the hundreds of thousands of real and potential Graceland pilgrims worldwide who understand that location as sacred ground and the anniversary of that tragic event of August 16, 1977—Elvis's early, unjust death—as a sacred day of remembrance.

Ground Zero

The roadside holy place shares much in common, but for scale, with Ground Zero, the New York City *locus sanctus* of the terrorist attack of September 11, 2001. Both give ceremonial expression to the localized sacred associated with unjust death. Being in the wrong place at the wrong time is part of the equation, but so also is victim-hood and an evil person or persons who have committed the unjust act that has, in effect, sanctified the location.

It is still not fully clear how much of and when Daniel Libeskind's World Trade Center master plan will be realized, with its multiple signature-architect skyscrapers, retail and cultural facilities, open green spaces, and transportation hub. The National September 11 Memorial and Museum, now under construction and scheduled to open soon, will honor those killed in the terrorist attacks of September 11, 2001, and February 26, 1993. According to its website, its four-fold mission is to "bear witness to the attacks, commemorate those who risked their lives to save others, recognize the thousands who survive and reflect on the unity and compassion shown in the aftermath." Its three main components, all within the World Trade Center Site, are: the Memorial, which opened on the 10th anniversary of the attack, and consists of two huge cascading pools set within the original footprints of the Twin Towers, listing around their perimeters the names of the victims; the Memorial Plaza, which is a contemplative green space with 300 swamp white

FIG. 47

oaks surrounding the pools; and the Memorial Museum, which descends gradually through successive exhibits to bedrock seven stories below its ground-level
entrance. The Museum will include both artifacts (relics) and photographs "pre-
senting the intimate stories of loss, compassion, reckoning, and recovery that are
central to our collective history." And, to the consternation of some of the victim's
families, the museum will include as well more than 9,000 unidentified bodily
remains at the bedrock level, behind a large inscription from Virgil's *Aeneid*: "No Day
Shall Erase You From the Memory of Time." To date, only 41% of the 2,752 victims
who died in the attacks at Ground Zero have been matched with their remains
and, like the Phnom Penh and Rwanda genocide museums (though unlike Yad
Vashem, in Jerusalem, where the ashes of Nazi victims are kept in a separate Hall
of Remembrance), the National September 11 Memorial and Museum will include
human remains as part of the visitor experience.

Among the largest relic/artifacts to be displayed in the Memorial Museum will
be the remains of the "survivors' staircase" that served as the escape route for hundreds of evacuees from #5 World Trade Center and the graffiti-covered "last column"
(#1001B) that was left standing as the site was cleared (fig. 47); the latter, which is
36 feet long and weighs 60 tons, was set in its future exhibit location on August 24,

2009, so that the museum could be built above and around it. On that solemn occasion, Sergeant James Buscemi of the Police Department's Emergency Service Unit was moved to say: "This is truly sacred ground here." Among the smallest relics to be exhibited is a victim's purse with a receipt from a family celebratory dinner in the Windows on the World restaurant at the top of the North Tower dated September 10.

Bits and pieces of the Twin Towers, some small and some enormous, have been sent around the globe to help establish regional surrogates for the tangible sanctity of Ground Zero. As of the 10th anniversary of the attack, more than one thousand pieces had been dispersed to museums, municipal buildings, and outdoor memorials around the United States, including 168 pieces to nearby New Jersey. When three giant steel beams, twisted and fused together during the collapse of the North Tower, arrived in Baltimore to become the centerpiece of the Maryland 9/11 memorial, which was dedicated on September 11, 2011, Governor Martin O'Malley called it "a sacred and holy relic."

The primary way for calling up memories of 9/11 is through photographs, some of the most powerful of which simply capture the front pages of newspapers from around the world dated September 12, 2001. In the Newseum in Washington, DC, a huge collage of these front pages provides the dramatic backdrop for an enormous relic of 9/11: the grotesquely-bent broadcast antenna from the North Tower (fig. 48). The dominant role of photography in the planned National September 11 Memorial and Museum will perpetuate an established memorializing tradition for Ground Zero. Soon after the attack, a display of photographs grew almost spontaneously nearby in SoHo, at 116 Prince Street; it

FIG.48

was called: *Here is New York, a Democracy of Photographs*. The word democracy was applicable because the display was simple and direct (no frames, no captions), and included both amateur and professional photographers.

That *ad hoc* Prince Street display inspired the first museum exhibition based on 9/11, which opened at the New York Historical Society on the 6th anniversary of the attack and ran until the following April; it was called: *Here is New York: Remembering 9/11*. This exhibition consisted of an enormous assembly of things photographic, including 1,500 prints from nearly 800 contributors and 500 video interviews. In addition, it had a small number of relics—debris retrieved by the FBI from the Fresh Kills Landfill on Long Island where the remains of the Twin Towers and everything in and around them destroyed in the attack were taken, including a scorched table clock stopped at 9:04, the moment of impact of the second plane. This was an exhibition, in its own words, "grounded in tangible things." On the 10th anniversary, the Prince Street/Historical Society photo documentary approach reappeared at the Westside Gallery in *Here is New York: Revisited*, while curators at MoMA PS1 in their *September 11* show retroactively empower George Segal's chalk-white figures and John Chamberlain's crushed-car sculptures with a new relic-like power.

The vast complex at Ground Zero will take time to build, and the relative success of these multiple ventures in achieving their multiple missions remains to be seen; in the meantime, though, two powerful 9/11 *loca sancta* already exist, one dating from the event itself and the other from September 2005.

The initial Ground Zero *locus sanctus* for pilgrimage and remembrance came into being within hours of the attack and it is unlikely ever to go away. It is tiny St. Paul's Chapel—the "Little Chapel that Stood"—just opposite the Twin Towers site toward the east. Initially, this was among the many places where relatives and friends put up flyers and "missing posters" pleading for information about their loved ones who worked in or intersected with the Twin Towers on that fateful September morning and had not been seen or heard from since. But when Broadway reopened in October 2001, the Chapel's wrought-iron fence quickly became the memorial *locus sanctus* of choice for Ground Zero pilgrims from around the world, who left their votive flags, T-shirts, hats, posters, letters, religious items, and, above all, their hand-written messages. At the same time, St. Paul's Chapel is the spot where the thousands of volunteers working in "the pit" in the months after the attack came at all hours of the day and night to seek physical and spiritual nourishment. The George Washington Pew became, for that time, the volunteer's podiatry station, where professionals would massage feet aching from hours of slogging work nearby at Ground Zero.

On the first anniversary of the attack, memorials and pilgrims from around the world were gathered on the sidewalks surrounding St. Paul's Chapel and its cemetery in a chaotic tableau of grief and remembrance perpetuating that of the first days after 9/11, with the addition by then of various souvenir vendors, including some selling snow globes of the Twin Towers, where the snow could only be understood as the storm of debris released by the collapsing skyscrapers. For the most part, these memorials were even more affectively powerful than roadside shrines, since few among those expressing their grief had physical remains over which to mourn and find closure. Most memorials were affixed to the fence, some still pleading 12 months after the fact for information on fate of those still unaccounted for, including:

ANN

NICOLE

NELSON

5'5"

Caucasian

Long Light Brown Hair

...

A Cantor Fitzgerald employee

104th floor—North Tower

World Trade Center

missing since 9-11-01

contact

the Nelsons

Stanley, ND 51984

....

MISSING FROM WORLD TRADE CENTER

FIG. 49

While the outside of St. Paul's Chapel has since been returned to its normal pre-attack state, the interior of the sanctuary has been transformed into a multi-faceted museum-shrine visited each day by thousands of Ground Zero pilgrims. A small mountain of votive badges left by firefighters and various law-enforcement officials seemingly from every nation on earth greets visitors immediately inside the entrance, as the first stop in a clockwise narrative around the sanctuary. Highlights on the circuit include an iron cross welded from remnants of a beam taken from the pit and a 14-inch-high Eucharistic chalice also fashioned from Twin Towers metal, whose base was given the form of a tree stump, recalling the remains of a large Sycamore in the Chapel's cemetery felled during the attack. There are scores of votive teddy bears, a simple cot standing in for the many that lined the walls of the sanctuary so that those working in the pit could rest, and boots left by veterans of the Iraq War. Officials at St. Paul's have also created a replica of the altar formerly just inside the entrance to the sanctuary, that in the months after 9/11 was the location where family and friends left hundreds of missing posters and mass cards for their loved ones (fig. 49). The pews are no longer aligned toward the front but rather are arranged in a circle around a stark altar table with another iron cross fashioned from debris taken out of the pit. Above and at the back of the sanctuary, affixed to the balcony, is one of more than 400 large canvases that over the months following 9/11 were hung on the Chapel's fence inviting written messages like this (fig. 50):

> *Go to GOD*
> *for comfort.*
> *HE will see you*
> *through. Paul Verble*
> *Edmund Fire Dept.*

Photographs accompanied by tangible things ennobled by their direct association with the attack are what make New York's second major 9/11 *locus sanctus,* the tiny Ground Zero Museum Workshop in the Meat Packing District, so powerful that its staff has found it necessary to place boxes of tissues around the room for those who break down during their visit. Among the most moving juxtapositions in this, the "Biggest Little Museum in New York," is one that includes a pre-attack photograph of the clock in the PATH workers' exercise room, stopped at 10:02 and 14 seconds, the moment when the North Tower collapsed, and the clock itself. At 1000 square feet, this mini-museum can accommodate just 24 visitors at a time, who must schedule in advance for their two-hour slot. Unlike the experience at St. Paul's

FIG. 50

FIG. 51

Chapel, that at the Ground Zero Museum Workshop is thoroughly tactile and gritty, including plenty of dirt and seemingly random debris from the pit (fig. 51). In the words of its brochure: "3-D installations, complete with dirt, will make you feel as if you 'were there' when the images were taken."

As at St. Paul's Chapel, there are crosses fashioned out of steel retrieved from Ground Zero, but the philosophy of the Ground Zero Museum Workshop is that visitors should touch at least some of the relic-artifacts in order fully to realize their power—thus the word workshop was added to its title. Visitors are told that just 1% of the glass from the Twin Towers survived the inferno of 9/11, that the thickest pieces among them came from near the top of the buildings where the winds were intense, and that the largest single section of Twin Tower glass that still exits is under the table where postcards and posters are for s d to note that the shards in the nearby display case have not had their rough edges polished off and have not even been cleaned, and that if the top were taken off that case visitors could breath in a bit of that acrid smell of burning metal that anyone who ever worked in the pit can never forget.

What little relief that can be found in this pressure-cooker experience comes in the audio stop for a case that includes, in addition to an intact set of screw drivers, a broken door handle, a deformed golf ball, a ripped stuffed doll, and a smashed beer can. The narrative over the headset informs visitors that beer cans just like this one were found in surprising abundance in the pit and that this particular brand, Rheingold, shut down operations in 1976. The explanation is simple: three decades before 9/11, as the Twin Towers were being built, construction workers were drinking at the site and hiding their crushed evidence in walls that soon would be sealed

The Ground Zero Museum Workshop is the creation of Gary Suson, formerly official photographer for the Uniformed Firefighters Association. Suson spent eight months as the only full-time, all-access photographer at Ground Zero—thus, the many photos of honor guards of firefighters carrying the flag-draped remains of one of their own up from the pit and the folded America flag in a display case affixed to the wall. Gary Suson narrates the 100-stop audio tour, conveying through it much of his own powerful feelings and recalling his own personal Ground Zero miracle. While gazing at a Suson photo of a ripped page from a Bible, visitors learn from the headset, in Suson's voice, that there came a point during his months in the pit when he simply could not go on, that the pain and grief he experienced daily could no longer be borne. And then he found this damaged Bible and his eyes fell on what was, in effect, its first page: Genesis 11, with the story of the Tower of Babel. That number and the word "tower" convinced Gary Suson that God had a mission for him and that he must go on photographing in the pit. Visitors also learn what brought the Ground Zero Museum Workshop into existence on the 4th anniversary of the attack. Gary Suson had no intention of creating a public display of his photographs and related artifacts until he visited Amsterdam and the home of Anne Frank. When he experienced onsite the story of the Jewish teenager who kept a diary of her life under Nazi occupation before she and her family were discovered and deported to the Bergen Belsen death camp, he realized he had an unrealized mission: to build this museum in the very building upon whose rooftop he stood on 9/11 to take photographs of the collapse of the Twin Towers. "I felt, if I could create something that would have an effect on people similar to the one the Anne Frank museum had on me, it could help people connect more to 9/11."

Auschwitz-Birkenau

Holocaust victims deported from Berlin are commemorated in the Jewish Quarter of that city near their former homes by German artist Gunter Demnig's inscribed

FIG. 52

brass "stumbling blocks" (*Stolpersteine*) that are set in the sidewalk slightly above grade in order to catch the toe of your shoe and thus your attention. (There are thousands of such memorial *Stolpersteinen* around Europe.) The Schneebau family—father Hermann, age 37, mother Jenny, age 35, 12-year-old daughter Thea and two-year-old son Victor—were deported together to Auschwitz in 1943 (fig. 52):

> *Here lived*
> *VICTOR SCHNEEBAU*
> *Born 1941*
> *Deported 1943*
> *Auschwitz*
> *Murdered*

The walls of apartment buildings fronting those sidewalks bear the names of deportees who lived there at the very location where their apartments once were. Nearby is a monument to mark the spot where Jews were collected for transport to the train station in the Grünewald from which they were deported; the loading platform beside the train tracks has an iron grate with a series of dates, the number of Jews deported on those dates, and their destination:

FIG. 53

27.3.1945

18 Jews

Berlin—Theresenstadt

Small stones are piled on the monument marking the collection spot in the city and a string of small stones lines the inscribed portion of iron grate at the train station; the practice is otherwise familiar from Jewish cemeteries. Like flowers, they indicate that someone has been there in a state of reverence and remembrance, but unlike flowers, those stones symbolize permanence.

Auschwitz-Birkenau, near Krakow in Poland, was the largest Nazi death camp. Each year hundreds of thousands visit the site, some in the mode of self-education and some in the mode of remembrance. The immense power of Auschwitz-Birkenau is conveyed in part through inspection of its inhuman living facilities and its machines of death, but mostly, its impact is achieved through the astounding volume of hair, shoes, toothbrushes, suitcases, *et cetera* that were taken from those who were to be killed and are now piled in store rooms (fig. 53). The inscribed suitcases have the power of contagion with the departed, as well as the human specificity of the otherwise antiseptic bronze stumbling stones back in Berlin, though nearly everything else in this factory for killing and in the supply line that fed it does not.

Hair, shoes, and toothbrushes are at once profoundly personal and at the same time anonymous. Each step in the journey from the Berlin apartments to the crematorium in Auschwitz has the hallowing of specificity of place; the train station adds to that a date and a number, and the apartments, stumbling blocks, and suitcases, the specificity of name, age, and date of deportation or arrival at Auschwitz. The suitcases, shoes, and toothbrushes have the added potency of having been held and used. The power they share to maintain memory and to evoke emotion is enormous, and draws on the same human reservoir of compassion and pity as does Ground Zero. Not surprisingly, given their abundance and potency, such anonymous personal items from the death camps have been integrated into Holocaust museum displays around the world.

The Daniel Libeskind master plan for lower Manhattan will be realized at the very site of the event; its role in capturing and memorializing 9/11 and in evoking the emotions associated with that day remains to be seen and experienced. The same architect designed the Jewish Museum in Berlin. Its location was determined not by what happened specifically there, but by the fact that it was commissioned to be contiguous with the existing Museum of the City of Berlin. Its power to tap into the emotions of its visitors is therefore not determined by its *locus sanctus* site or by the presence of relics, nor even because of the Jewish symbolism that the architect embedded throughout the building, including its very footprint, a contorted Star of David (which can only be recognized from above). Rather, the building's disorienting angles, confined spaces, and outdoor pillar-garden that at once invites exploration and traps the explorers, together create an effect that leaves some visitors weeping and nearly all visitors profoundly moved.

Loca Sancta for Secular Charismatic Martyrs

The desire to be close to the spot where "it" happened draws pilgrims to the Grassy Knoll at Dealey Plaza in Dallas where John F. Kennedy was assassinated on November 22, 1963; to the balcony outside room #306 of the Lorraine Motel in Memphis where Martin Luther King, Jr. was shot on April 4, 1968; to Pre's Rock along Skyline Boulevard in Eugene, Oregon, where famed long-distance runner Steve Prefontaine died in a car crash on May 30, 1975; to room #158 in the Corpus Christi Days Inn where the Tejano singing sensation Selena was murdered on March 31, 1997; and to pillar #13 in the tunnel beneath Place de l'Alma in Paris where Princess Diana and her boyfriend Dodi perished in a gruesome car accident on August 31, 1997. The Sixth Floor Museum in Dallas, which includes the window from which Lee Harvey Oswald fired the fatal bullets and the 26-seconds of Abraham Zapruder's Kodakrome II showing their impact, engenders a profound sense of time collapse back to November 22, 1963, especially for those of us old enough to remember. The same time collapse, though in this case to April 4, 1968, is achieved at the National Civil Rights Museum in the Lorraine Motel, whose compelling story line ultimately leads visitors to the motel's second floor and into room #306—and then, finally, out on to the very balcony where Martin Luther King was assassinated. There, pilgrims struggle to identify the window in the rooming house opposite where the rifle shot was fired, as if mimicking King's frantically gesturing entourage, as captured in the famous photograph taken seconds after the assassination.

No pilgrim inscriptions are permitted on the walls of the Lorraine Motel though they are at least tolerated on the wooden fence at the top of the Grassy

FIG. 54

FIG. 55
FIG. 56

Knoll and on virtually any flat and accommodating surface near the entry to Diana's fatal tunnel (fig. 54). Conspiracy theories, which appear occasionally among the inscriptions at Ground Zero, are prominent at Place de l'Alma and dominant at the Grassy Knoll, where pilgrims still draw conspiratorial inspiration by position-ing themselves behind the fence where they are convinced the second gunman stood. The inscriptions left by JFK and Princess Di visitors lay bare a collective struggle to accept the truth that a char-ismatic figure can die in a mundane way: in a car accident, at the hands of a politically crazed sniper, or, for Elvis, from a lethal combination of prescrip-tion drugs. There is a shared predisposition to believe that there must instead be a grand conspiracy at work, drawing on powerful evil forces. Only something very big could take Princess Diana from us, not the simple fact that her driver was strung out on alcohol and drugs.

The distorted thinking of these conspiracy theorists is fueled by a powerful need we all share to give purpose to things and events in our lives; the bigger the thing or event, the bigger the purpose. This predisposition toward magical, "teleo-logical" reasoning (from the Greek word *telos,* meaning "end" or "purpose") has been identified by psychologists as already fully formed in small children, who readily assign functions to natural phenomena, such as clouds, which are "for rain." So again, it boils down to what evolutionary biology has hardwired in our brains: all things Elvis (Diana, JFK, Tupac, *et cetera*) must have meaning, direction, and pur-pose; it is simply up to us to figure out what that is.

Not so far away from pillar #13 in Paris is the gravesite of singer Jim Morrison in Père-Lachaise Cemetery. This is the sacred site of the singer's internment but not of his death, which took place on July 3, 1971, in a Paris apartment bathtub from a drug overdose. There is no museum experience in the cemetery to engender a sense of time collapse back to the summer of 1971 for Morrison pilgrims; quite the opposite, the dominant emotion at eventually finding Jim's gravesite in the cemetery's maze of 63 acres of ornate monuments is one of frustration—or perhaps, for true believers, one of triumph. Votive inscriptions are not permitted on the nearby tombs in this solemn public venue and there are ever-present security guards to ensure good behavior. But the *Doors'* cannabis and booze generation and their descendents are nothing if not resourceful, so every now and then a flurry of hastily-scribbled notes will appear, only to be cleaned away in short order. These will typically include attestations of devotion to Jim's memory and occasionally desperate assertions that Jim Morrison and not Elvis Presley is "The King" (fig. 55). On the other hand, pilgrim votives are, for now at least, allowed on a forlorn tree near Jim's tomb, where they have become so dense as to be unreadable—and are in some locations intermixed with votive candle wax (fig. 56).

FIG. 57
FIG. 58

Like the Ascension Mount and Chimayo, the main take-away at the gravesite of Jim Morrison is dirt (fig. 57), that is periodically replenished to fill the open rectangle frame above the singer's tomb. Morrison pilgrims' other favorite thing to take with them is a rubbing—a simple sacred transfer realized by way of a pencil rubbed across a piece of paper set against the raised letters of Jim's bronze grave marker that bears the words in Greek: "True to His Own Spirit" (fig. 58). There is

nothing new here; in the later 6th century the Piacenza pilgrim witnessed similar acts of pilgrim piety in Jerusalem, where the faithful sought out the Column of the Flagellation that bore the imprint of the hands of Jesus. They would take a strip of cloth and set it against the sacred imprint and then mark it, making permanent and transferable the sanctity of the *locus sanctus*; these strips would then be worn around the neck, bringing cures from "any kind of disease."

Graceland Stands Apart

What makes Graceland unique among both religious and secular *loca sancta*—a Category 5 hurricane, a 9.5 earthquake on the Richter Scale—is the fact that nearly all the defining characteristics of a holy place, whether ancient or modern, whether religious or secular, are concentrated there. Even the Church of the Holy Sepulchre cannot match that. Not only was this Elvis's home for the last 20 years of his life, it was the site of his death and funeral, and it is the location of his body. Graceland is itself a relic and is filled with relics, some of which were on site when Elvis died and some of which have been returned over the years.

By contrast, John F. Kennedy was killed in Dallas and is entombed in Arlington, Virginia, far from his boyhood home in Massachusetts. The material remains of JFK's life are prized, commanding top prices at celebrity memorabilia auctions, but they are dispersed all over the world. Martin Luther King, Jr. was killed in Memphis, but his tomb is in Atlanta near his boyhood home and his church. Princess Diana's death *locus* in Paris is difficult and dangerous to get to and very far from her tomb, which is set on an island in a small lake in England. Harvey Milk was killed in San Francisco's City Hall, his apartment and photo business are in the Castro District of the city, and, while there are relics there to commemorate his life and martyrdom, Milk was cremated and his ashes dispersed. Selena's *loca sancta*, including her grave, her museum with her life-size statue as *Mirador de la Flor* and her Porsche, her parents' home, and the site of her murder at a Days Inn Motel are all in her hometown of Corpus Christi, Texas, but they are scattered around the city. Neverland, near Santa Barbara, is bereft of nearly everything related to Michael Jackson's time there. Moreover, Michael Jackson died in a rented house in the Holmby Hills neighborhood of Los Angeles, was eulogized miles away at the Staples Center, and his body is now locked away and inaccessible in the Grand Mausoleum at Forest Lawn Cemetery in Glendale, which is far from both the death and funeral locations.

By contrast with Neverland, Graceland is and always has been a vast repository of Elvis relics. It gathers in one place all the everyday items associated with Elvis that parallel the everyday items from the life of Jesus that the Piacenza pilgrim encountered at various locations in the Holy Land, including his holy cradle and swaddling cloth in Bethlehem and his childhood schoolbook in Nazareth. Graceland is not only the fully furnished Elvis house, it is the Elvis tomb, and, though off-limits to visitors, the place of Elvis martyrdom, in the form of the second floor master bathroom, over the front door, which remains pretty much as it was the day Elvis died there. In the Trophy Building, between the Elvis house and the Meditation Garden with the Elvis tomb, visitors are invited to contemplate a cornucopia of dazzling Elvis relics, mostly items of clothing: a gold lamé suit and white bucks of the '50s (fig. 59), various theatrical outfits from his movie years of the '60s, and finally, a series of increasingly elaborate caped and rhinestone-studded jumpsuits from the

FIG. 59 FIG. 60

FIG. 61

touring and Vegas concerts of the '70s. Among these is the most striking relic of all: Elvis's famous jumpsuit from the *Elvis—Aloha from Hawaii* concert of 1973, with its massive eagle-encrusted trophy belt (fig. 60).

Across the street from Graceland Mansion, the tour of the tactilely-empowered continues with relics of the King's transportation life: Elvis cars (fig. 61) and the big Elvis plane, the *Lisa Marie*, incongruously parked along a suburban boulevard. Some years back, the Elvis bus, which is privately owned, was reclaimed and so now can only be engaged vicariously, by way of photographs. As for the King's private life as father and spiritualist, in the late '80s the Sincerely Elvis Museum in Graceland Plaza displayed a variety of Elvis's household items, among them Lisa Marie's crib and his own spiritual bookshelf, including Kahlil Gibran's *The Prophet*. Finally, this treasure trove of charismatically-infused "stuff" (as fans call it) from Elvis's adult life gathered in Memphis is complemented with relics from his childhood years just two hours away in the new museum adjacent to Elvis's birth house in Tupelo; on display there is the wooden-handled claw hammer with which his father Vernon built the now legendary shotgun shack in which the King of Rock 'n' Roll was born.

Like the Church of the Holy Sepulchre, and Jerusalem more generally, Graceland and its various complementary pilgrimage destinations have been

FIG. 62

replicated around the world. A tiny complex of dollhouse-like buildings called "Mini-Graceland" (a.k.a. "Elvis City"), which together approximate Graceland, Tupelo, and various Presley performance venues, was for many years maintained as a popular pilgrimage/tourist destination in Roanoke, Virginia (fig. 62); its scale is suggested by the fact that a hospital emesis bowl serves as the Mansion's swimming pool. Jimmy Carter was among Mini-Graceland's thousands of visitors, some of whom would gather on the evening of August 15 for their own mini candlelight vigil. The complex was created by Don and Kim Epperly in 1987 on a sloping property adjacent to their home at the base of Mill Mountain. For years thereafter they would add an enhancing element or two annually, and Mrs. Epperly would daily dress the little Elvis doll in a different outfit. Unfortunately, the couple's declining health in the later '90s led to a corresponding decline in the architectural fabric of Mini-Graceland, which from the beginning was fully exposed to the elements and in 2005 was partially crushed by a falling tree during a storm. Happily, Don and Kim's middle-aged son Mike decided the next year to clean up the grounds, so Mini-Graceland's future is now a bit brighter.

The most recent entrant in the field of off-site Gracelands—one that, unlike Mini-Graceland, cannot be integrated into an overland pilgrimage to Memphis—opened in mid-April 2011 in Randers, Denmark; appropriately, it is called Randers

FIG. 63

Graceland (fig. 63). The brainchild of Henrick Knudsen, an Elvis fan from way back, Denmark's version of Graceland cost nearly $5,000,000, and though an "exact replica" of Graceland Mansion, it is in fact twice the size in order to accommodate the Elvis Museum, housing 6,000 Elvis artifacts, and the Highway 51 Diner. There, one can enjoy an "EP's All Time Favourite" sandwich (peanut butter and mashed banana on fried white bread) followed by a portion of "Sweet Tooth" banana pudding (again, the "King's Favourite") served with whipped cream—both for just under $20. Knudsen expects somewhere between 50,000 and 125,000 visitors annually, and in order to keep them enthralled, he has arranged many social events and excursions, which are listed on Randers Graceland's website, including "Cadillacs Tomorrow!"

The most unusual Elvis remote shrine/museum, until it was recently dismantled and sold, could be found along interstate #70 about 45 miles west of St. Louis. Called the Elvis is Alive Museum (fig. 64), it was maintained for nearly two decades as an expression of Baptist minister Bill Beeny's conviction that Elvis is still alive; thus its name, and thus its replication of a portion of Graceland Mansion at the time of Elvis's (reputed) funeral. To demonstrate how easily even Elvis's friends might have been fooled by a rubber dummy, Reverend Beeny—who is also an Elvis look-alike (fig. 65)—concocted his own funeral room to approximate the setting and experience of the open Presley casket in the Mansion's living room in August 1977. Neither signage nor a guide was necessary to feel the persuasive power of the Elvis is Alive Museum. The raw concrete floor and the yellowed clippings from the tabloids taped to the walls were only minor distractions as visitors were drawn inexorably forward, toward the funeral room. There, at the back of the tiny museum, visitors encountered an ensemble of plastic flower arrangements framing an open casket. Coming closer, they were confronted with what was certainly a rubber Elvis (fig. 66), seemingly with acne, and were invited in that moment to empathize with those gullible friends and fans who processed past the King's open casket, only to mistake rubber for flesh and plastic for hair. To quote Reverend Beeny: "It doesn't look like Elvis, but neither did the guy in the casket." Despite its appearance, the Beeny casket dummy must have had some power over the museum's visitors; so many plastic eyebrows were pulled off his rubber Elvis that Beeny eventually painted on replacements.

In Holly Springs, halfway between Memphis and Tupelo, is Graceland Too, Paul "The World's Biggest Elvis Fan" MacLeod's phantasmagorical home and

FIG. 64

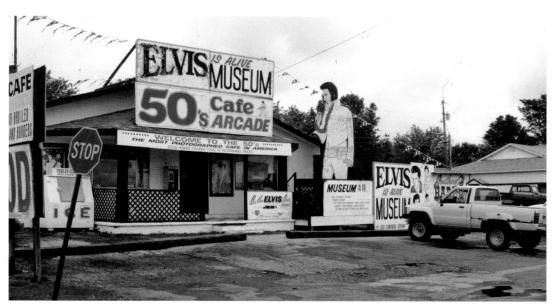

FIG. 65

homage to the King of Rock 'n' Roll. Open to visitors 24/7, for $5 and a loud knock, Graceland Too ("The Mecca of Elvis World") is only a few blocks off the main square of Holly Springs (fig. 67). It both self-identifies and marginal-izes itself in its staid surroundings by its (sometimes) pink paint job and its Graceland-like portico and paired plaster lions (fig. 68). Out back is a work-in-progress stage set for Jailhouse Rock, including a high-backed wooden electric chair enveloped in wires and chains. Paul's wife left him ("It's either Elvis or me"), and his son, christened Elvis Aaron Presley MacLeod, is far away in New York City, "tak-ing care of business" there; this means that Paul alone gives the house tour, which typically lasts at least 90 minutes, but once, according to Paul, it went on for 12 hours.

Paul claims to have welcomed 100,000 visitors over the years, including Matthew Broderick, Steven Segal, and Tom Brokow, whose pictures and those of thousands of other Graceland Too pilgrims are affixed in rows to the walls of one of the six downstairs rooms. Paul's MacLeod's TV room is full of monitors, old TV

FIG. 66

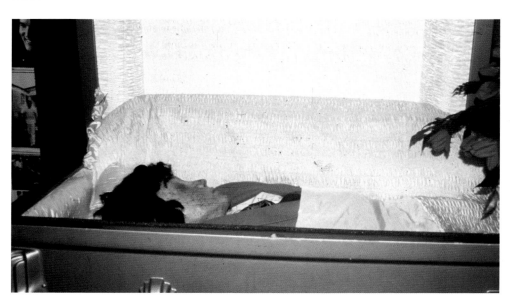

FIG. 67

Guides, and elaborate recording equipment running day
and night in order to capture
any chance reference to Elvis,
no matter how mundane and
fleeting, that Paul then documents by hand in one of his
hundreds of Elvis notebooks.
Among Paul MacLeod's vast
and varied collection, which
he claims numbers ten million

FIG 68

Elvis items (including lots of wrappers from Reese's Peanut Butter Cups, which Elvis
loved and Paul loves) is "the most valuable recording of all time," Elvis's first, for
which George W. Bush offered, says Paul, $10,000,000, as well as bottles of Elvis
wine that once sold for $12.95 and are now worth, he claims, $10,000 each. Paul
also proudly displays petals from the first flower laid on Elvis's grave, which he says
he stole.

III.
GRACELAND VISITORS *as* PILGRIMS

Pilgrims are the life-blood of any holy place. Without them a *locus sanctus* is merely an empty, historical monument. Contrast Graceland and Mount Vernon, where the graves of George and Martha are an afterthought, and the local hero's death day, December 14, is all but meaningless. In the eyes of the faithful, the tomb of a saint was and is still understood to be much more than mere tangible evidence of the historical reality of that individual; it is a sacred point of intersection between the physical and the metaphysical, between earth and heaven. (So, too, of course, are the *loca sancta* associated with biblical events.) The soul of the saint is believed to dwell there and being nearby (*ad sanctus*) is to be in the company of one's invisible friend. Conversely, to be separated from the tomb is to be apart from that friend, and the remedy is pilgrimage.

(Thus, the remains of Rudolf Hess, Hitler's deputy, were recently dug up and disposed of, and his grave marker destroyed, because their location in the small Bavarian town of Wunsiedel had become a pilgrimage destination for Neo-Nazis on Hess' death day, August 17. And thus, Osama bin Laden's body was dropped into the Indian Ocean.)

Within a few generations of the transfer of the Empire's capital by Emperor Constantine from Rome to Constantinople in 330, the eastern Mediterranean began to come alive with pious travelers. Among the first was Constantine's mother Helen, who traveled to Palestine at her son's request to build and dedicate churches located at the sacred sites identified with the birth, death, and ascension of Christ. Tens of thousands were to follow in a mobilization of body and spirit that grew uninterrupted until the Arab conquest of the eastern Mediterranean lands in the 7th century. These early pilgrims were drawn not only to those places in Palestine associated with the life of Christ and enshrined by Constantine, but also to sites in Egypt, Syria, Asia Minor, and Greece made sacred by their association with the relics of saints or with living holy men like Saint Simeon.

Holy men and women, living or dead, and the miracle-working objects associated with them, like Simeon's column, were secondary in the development of early pilgrimage to holy sites associated with the Bible, most of which were in Palestine. Old Testament sites greatly outnumbered those associated with the New and included such stunning and remote locations as Mount Sinai, where Moses is believed to have received the Ten Commandments. Not surprisingly, however, places linked to the life, miracles, and Passion of Christ enjoyed the greatest popularity, and at the head of the list was Jerusalem, which could claim half a dozen of the most significant shrines in Christendom. From the reign of Constantine in the early 4th century to the incursions by Persia, and then the Arab conquest of the region in the first half of the 7th century, Jerusalem became one vast pilgrim complex, with an established circuit of sites, scores of churches, shrines, and relics, huge hospices, and tens of thousands of visitors—all of whom were dramatically orchestrated into great citywide processions on the most important days in the church calendar. For example, on Palm Sunday, masses of pilgrims would wave palm fronds before the bishop as he came down from the Mount of Olives on a donkey in imitation of Jesus, chanting as he passed: "Blessed is he who comes in the name of the Lord" (Matthew 21:9).

Who were these early pilgrims? The 5th-century historian Theodoret of Cyrrhus gives an eyewitness account of the huge, multiethnic crowds drawn to Saint Simeon the Stylite:

> *Not only do the inhabitants of our part of the world flock together, but also Ishmaelites, Persians, Armenians subject to them, Iberians, Homerites, and men even more distant than these; and there came many inhabitants of the extreme west, Spaniards, Britons, and the Gauls who live between them. Of Italy it is superfluous to speak.*

A pilgrim might be from the other end of the Mediterranean or from the next town. Depending on the time of year, the ratio of out-of-towners to locals could be much higher, as in Jerusalem at Easter. Perhaps the simplest criterion for identifying a pilgrim is that it is someone who has interrupted his or her normal life activities with the religiously-motivated goal of visiting a holy site, whether nearby or far away. But eventually, religiously-motivated travel to Jerusalem and the great *loca sancta* of the eastern Mediterranean simply became, in the words of the renowned Byzantinist, Cyril Mango, "the thing to do."

Major biblical sites and famous miracle-working saints and their relics were the great attractions that set the early Christian world in motion. Each by itself would merit a pilgrim's journey. Yet once on holy soil, the pious traveler was offered an abundant menu of lesser attractions that were worth at least a detour. Around 570, the Piacenza pilgrim entered Palestine by way of Ptolemais (modern Acre/Acco), keeping a detailed diary as he made his way south toward Jerusalem. He stopped first at Diocaesarea (Zippori) to see the chair in which the Virgin sat during the Annunciation and then went on to Cana to touch the two surviving water jugs whose contents Jesus had miraculously turned into wine. From there he was off just four miles or so to Nazareth where, among other things, he saw preserved in the local synagogue the book in which Jesus had as a child written his ABCs. And then he was off again another seven miles to climb Mount Tabor, the site of the Transfiguration.

The pilgrim's journey also included many local curiosities that would delight or shock any foreigner. Among these were the one-pound dates that the Piacenza pilgrim picked and carted home from Jericho, and the Ethiopians he encountered in the Negev Desert, who "had their nostrils split, their ears cut, boots on their feet, and rings on their toes." His journey was slow, not only because of his many stops but also because of the very nature of travel at that period. Egeria, a Spanish noblewoman who made her pilgrimage to Palestine around 380, beginning her journey "right from the other end of the earth," spent more than four years away from home, at least one of which was fully consumed in travel. There were rest houses for these traveling strangers and for the sick. The elaborate architectural remains at Saint Simeon's shrine, with its triumphal arch on the route leading up to the column, suggest that the movement of crowds of pilgrims was sometimes dramatically orchestrated. A pilgrim might pack a variety of travel aids, including scriptures for appropriate readings at each site, an *Onomasticon* ("list of places") to give the modern, local names for biblical places, letters of introduction and transit, and perhaps even maps and guidebooks. The *Breviarius* ("short account") *of Jerusalem* from the early 6th century is written in a crisp and efficient style; it reveals its function as a pilgrim's guidebook in its opening words:

> *This city [Jerusalem] is set on a mountain. In the center of the city is the Basilica of Constantine. As one goes into the basilica itself there is a chamber on the left....*

Pilgrimage has always been intertwined with tourism, even in the days of the early Christian saints. Undoubtedly most of the 600,000 annual visitors to Graceland come in the tourist mode, though many of them may eventually experience there at least a vague sense of the localized sacred. And certainly, many among that minority whose initial travel aims are closer to those of the Piacenza pilgrim might still be distracted by such local Memphis curiosities as Mud Island, Beale Street, and baby back ribs at The Rendevous. The trick is to disentangle both statistically and qualitatively the pilgrim attitude from the tourist attitude, even as they coexist in the same person. A *locus sanctus* is identifiable not only by a set of physical characteristics (the death site, the sacred body, relics, *et cetera*) but also by what people believe about the place and do in relationship to it. This is Max Weber's affectual action notion again: as the charismatic is defined by how he is treated as endowed by his audience, so also his *locus sanctus* will be defined. Moreover, the history of religiously-motivated travel to holy places inside and outside of Christianity suggests several activity-defined criteria for identifying the pilgrim and thus, by extension, the holy place. These include the interrelated concepts of sacred time and sacred itinerary, *communitas, mimesis*, public and private rituals, relics, sacred souvenirs, and votives.

Sacred Time

The travel schedule of the tourist is dictated primarily by vacation time and the seasons, whereas that of the pilgrim is dictated by the yearly calendar of holy days associated with the sanctification of the destination site. The Piacenza pilgrim goes to the Jordan River on January 6, the day each year when the Baptism of Christ is commemorated there; similarly, since the earliest centuries of Christianity,

Bethlehem has been the preferred pilgrimage destination for December 25 and Jerusalem for Holy Week. This is so because in the eyes of the faithful a holy day, within the unending yearly cycle of sacred remembrances, is an occasion of complete time collapse. To be in the Church of the Holy Sepulchre on any day is to be proximate to the sacred, but to be there on Good Friday is to be there at the Crucifixion. Of course sacred time exists independent of sacred locale in Easter services worldwide, but to be in Jerusalem for those services is to compound the intensity of the spiritual encounter. Sacred experience is in this respect a function of both the "where" and the "when." This belief lies at the heart of what it is to be human: surviving relatives return to their roadside shrine on the anniversary of the accident; Ground Zero is a special destination on September 11; and many of us visit the graves of our parents on their death days, just as our Roman counterparts did two millennia ago. Hindus have the *Shraddah* ceremony for yearly remembrance of the dead and, since Talmudic times, Judaism has had the *Yahrzeit*, when the mourner's *Kaddish* prayer is recited three times and the *Yarhzeit* candle burns for 24 hours. A recent secular yearly remembrance was initiated on June 25, 2010, when local media in San Diego, Philadelphia, and New York coordinated mass Thriller dances on the anniversary of Michael Jackson's death.

Contributing to a powerful sensation of time collapse during Elvis Week are the steamy weather, the nighttime crowds on Elvis Presley Boulevard, and the ubiquitous Elvis tribute artists. Moreover, there is ever-present outdoor Elvis music at Graceland during Elvis Week, supplied by Sirius Satellite Radio, on location. This is complemented and intensified by the periodic rebroadcast on Elvis-era radio station 56-WHBQ of the heart-wrenching interview with Vernon Presley on the afternoon of August 16, 1977, shortly after Elvis had been pronounced dead at Baptist Memorial Hospital. A comparably powerful emotional sense of the moment is achieved in the Sixth Floor Museum at Dealey Plaza in Dallas, through a combination of the Zupruder film and repeated rebroadcast of CBS anchor Walter Cronkite breaking into the popular mid-day soap opera *As the World Turns* to report that President Kennedy had been shot, and then, just minutes later, looking at the clock and on the verge of emotional collapse, announcing that Kennedy had died from his wounds "some 38 minutes ago."

FIG. 69

Disney World is fully booked in mid-March because this is when school children have their spring vacation and when the weather in Florida is especially attractive. By contrast, Chimayo is most active during Holy Week, and Graceland's peak activity is always in mid-August during Elvis Week. The second most important Elvis holiday is January 8, his birthday, and after that comes Christmas and then Mother's Day, reflecting Elvis's deep family ties and his reverence for his mother Gladys. And the list goes on: calendars are sold highlighting three or four days every month of special Elvis significance, including the birthday of Lisa Marie (February 1), the day Elvis was discharged from the army (March 5), Elvis's wedding anniversary (May 1), and the day Elvis's divorce became official (October 9).

Sacred Itinerary

Tupelo

The organizing criterion for a tourist's itinerary might be Civil War battlefields, theme parks with roller coasters, three-star restaurants or campgrounds. By contrast, the pilgrim has always organized his or her itinerary around *loca sancta* that are at once secondary but complementary to the prime holy place that motivated the trip in the first place. The Piacenza pilgrim took many sacred detours and, like most other Holy Land travelers then and since, made use of specially designed maps and guidebooks both to acquaint himself with appropriate ancillary destinations and to help get him there. His counterpart Graceland pilgrim will likely have, in addition to the site map for Graceland, something like the Red Line *Map and Guide, with Historical Addresses to Elvis Presley.*

The Red Line *Map* will point the Presley pilgrim southward on interstate #78 about 100 miles to the Elvis birth shrine in Tupelo, Mississippi. The prime relic among the secondary Elvis *loca sancta* is father Vernon's 1934 shotgun shack (fig. 69), where Elvis was born in the early morning hours of January 8, 1935. (A shotgun shack is so named because a shotgun blast can enter the home through the front door and exit through the back door without hitting anything.) Encircling the Elvis birth house is the Walk of Life, comprising a series of dated granite blocks tracing each year of Elvis's life from 1935 to 1977; it begins with: "Elvis was born here at 4:35 am on January 8." The intent is to give fans an opportunity to "stop and reflect on memorable events in Elvis's life, as well as their own." This is again, depending on the day of your visit, a compounding convergence of sacred time and sacred place. Much has changed in this part of Tupelo since the Presley family moved out (because Vernon couldn't pay the rent) 2 ½ years after Elvis was born. The neighboring shacks are gone, elegant shrubbery now surrounds the Presley house, and its interior has been refurbished with a bed, pot belly stove, kitchen table, *et cetera* of the sort that would once have been part of the Presleys' spare domestic ensemble. Visitors are received warmly by an enthusiastic volunteer eager to supply all the detailed information about young Elvis, Gladys, and Vernon that a true Elvis fan will likely not need. And while visitors are certainly not encouraged to do so, touching (e.g., the stove) is not expressly forbidden; moreover, unlike Graceland Mansion, the Elvis birth house is not closely monitored. Out back is a 1939 green Plymouth sedan, a replica of the car the Presley family drove when they left Tupelo for Memphis in 1948, in the words of the inscribed commemorative granite block nearby "seeking a 'Better Living'." While it is not at all obvious to most visitors, it is subtly meaningful that the Plymouth has been parked facing northwest, in the direction of Memphis.

FIG. 70

Over the years, the park-like space surrounding the Presley house (the Elvis
Presley Birthplace Complex), which is a Mississippi Historic Landmark, has been
enriched with a gift shop offering more than 2,000 souvenir items and a Story Wall
with educational signage devoted to Elvis's early life, as told by some of his childhood friends; the brochure assures visitors that all of the texts are "original and
unedited." Just to the left of the Story Wall is the Fountain of Life. Above are 13
waterspouts representing the 13 years Elvis spent in Tupelo; they spill over granite,
a very hard stone "symbolizing the enduring power of strong values learned during
his formative years." By contrast, the 29 lower spouts, which stand for the years
Elvis spent in Memphis, flow over limestone, a much softer stone "symbolizing the
softer, better conditions of Elvis's life as an entertainer." Just behind the Story Wall
and Fountain of Life is the Elvis Presley Memorial Chapel, the site's "place of meditation," complete with stained-glass windows, oak pews donated by fan clubs from
around the world, and one of Elvis's Bibles resting on the original pulpit from the
First Assembly of God Pentecostal Church; it is opened to the Book of Revelations.

That one-room church where the Presley family attended services has itself
recently been moved to the grounds (fig. 70). There, visitors are invited to sit in the
very pews that the Presleys sat in and experience the Pentecostal services of the

'40s through a multi-media presentation. They also learn, in the words of Brother Frank Smith, that "Elvis was fascinated with music and the prospect of learning to play the guitar" and that his voice was "a gift from God." According to the accepted *vita* narrative, Brother Smith taught little Elvis just three cords, which was all he needed to sing *Old Shep*. Combined with the gift shop is the Elvis Presley Museum, which explores the world of baby and young Elvis, including such relics as the hammer that Vernon used to build the shotgun birth house, comic books (specifically, *Captain Marvel Jr.*) of the sort little Elvis would have read, and an explanation of what a Pentecostal church may have contributed to Elvis's musical formation in terms of gyrations and rapturous singing, and in terms of healing, through the observation on the plaque that among many Pentecostals, healing is practiced "by the laying on of hands." (Not only are Jerry Lee Lewis and televangelist Jimmy Swaggart cousins, they are, like their contemporary Elvis, both products of their Pentecostal upbringing.)

FIG. 71

One of the favorite photo opportunities in the park is the *Elvis at 13* life-size bronze statue that was added in 2002 at the suggestion of an Elvis fan from Ireland (fig. 71). The work, which shows young Elvis in the oversized overalls and the plain shoes of poverty, is rich in iconographic import; according to the Elvis Presley Birthplace brochure, the sculptor "envisioned Elvis walking to the Tupelo Overlook where he would sit and play his guitar and dream of a better life." Even the statue's position has meaning; in the words of that same brochure: "The statue is positioned with the chapel on his right and the museum to his left symbolizing the strong spiritual values he learned in Tupelo and the challenge of materialism he would eventually face in Memphis."

The Red Line *Map* or any other variety of travel aids will direct the ardent Presley pilgrim from the Birth Place Complex to the Tupelo Hardware Co., where he will be invited to stand in the very spot where Elvis stood on his 9th birthday, when his mother Gladys persuaded him to accept a guitar for his present instead of the bicycle he had his eye on. Then, halfway back on the return trip to Memphis, Elvis pilgrims may choose to make a short detour to Holly Springs, which is not only rich in the flavor of the *antebellum* South, it is home of Graceland Too, which may well

FIG. 72

consume an entire afternoon. After Holly Springs and Graceland Too, the truly devoted pilgrim might wish to take a final pre-Memphis detour 340 miles west on interstate #40 to Fort Smith, Arkansas, there to enjoy a new, tertiary Elvis *locus sanctus*: the Chaffee Barbershop Museum, at Fort Chaffee, where Private Elvis was inducted into the Army and began his basic training. The Chaffee Barbershop Museum, which ranks near the bottom on the Fort Smith website's list of local historic attractions, marks the spot where Elvis got his military buzz cut on March 25, 1958, "the haircut heard 'round the world." Or, as Elvis said, when asked what he thought of giving up his famous hairstyle: "Hair today, gone tomorrow!" Who could then have guessed that 51 years later a clump of that Kingly hair scooped up off the barbershop floor that day would fetch $15,000 at auction?

FIG. 73

Memphis

Back in Memphis, a variety of Elvis maps will offer several detours to such important local sites as Lauderdale Courts, Elvis's first Memphis home; Humes High School (now Humes Middle School), the place of Elvis's education and sports life; Sun Records, Elvis's first recording studio; and, in former times, Chenault's Restaurant, "where Elvis and his guests would have hamburgers in the sealed off back room." Everywhere on the tour there will be an intense feeling of Elvis's presence, heightened by sacred contact: one sits on the very stoop at Lauderdale Courts where Elvis once sat as he sang to his first girlfriend, Betty McMann. In the '80s, a visit to Humes High would include the screening of a short film in the auditorium documenting the King's school life, including his bench-warmer role on the Humes High football team: Elvis was the scrawny kid with the narrow shoulders in the front row on the left. After the film, pilgrims were invited to contemplate a partially reconstructed Elvis classroom, and even touch the Elvis football uniform hanging in the Elvis locker (fig. 72), and then write a message to the King on the Elvis blackboard. The Memphis Elvis tour will necessarily include the tiny Sun Records studio (fig. 73), where fans can hear and experience, as if it were happening right then for the first time, the excitement of the *Million Dollar Quartet*, the jam session that

FIG. 74

resulted from the chance encounter there on December 4, 1956, of Elvis, Johnny Cash, Carl Perkins, and Jerry Lee Lewis. The CD is available for purchase in the adjacent café, as is a variety of Sun Records, T-shirts, and peanut butter and mashed banana sandwiches, Elvis's favorite lunch treat.

Such destinations are, of course, a prelude and complement to the Graceland experience *per se*; those small clusters of Elvis devotees in each of those secondary and tertiary Elvis *loca sancta* eventually converge on Graceland Mansion, the Elvis mega-shrine (fig. 74). There, pilgrims and tourists in vast numbers rub shoulders daily in the Estate's exquisitely choreographed no-touch encounter with the life and death settings of the King—*sans*, of course, access to the second-floor bedroom and adjoining bathroom, where Elvis expired on the toilet. The Graceland ticket office, in Graceland Plaza just opposite Music Gates, usually has a line, which is good, because there are tough decisions to be made. The threshold ticket, the "Mansion Tour," which includes only the audio-tour of Graceland Mansion and grounds, is the cheapest ($30 in 2010) and the quickest, at a recommended 1½ to 2 hours. But the "Platinum Tour" costs only about 10% more and offers 2½ to 3 hours of all things Elvis, including many core attractions in and around Graceland Plaza that are not part of the simple Mansion Tour. Among these are Elvis's two custom airplanes, featuring, in the larger *Lisa Marie*, gold-plated seatbelt buckles, gold-flecked sinks, and, on its enormous tail fin, Elvis's TCB motto with lightning bolt in gold letters (fig. 75). South on the same side of Elvis Presley Boulevard, at the far end of the Plaza, is Elvis's Automobile Museum, with its 33 vehicles, including the John Deere 4010 that Elvis used to tidy up the 14-acre grounds of Graceland and, on a concrete slab out front, a green Cadillac convertible with white side-wall tires. The Platinum Tour offers access as well to several smaller ticketed exhibits around Graceland Plaza and Graceland Crossing (the smaller complex just north of the Plaza), including the Private Presley Exhibit, with such relic/artifacts as Elvis's foot locker and fatigues—again, not accessible to touch.

The top-priced Graceland ticket is the "Elvis Entourage VIP Tour." It is twice as expensive as the Platinum Tour but is still rated at 2 ½ to 3 hours and offers such marginal incremental benefits as front-of-the-line Mansion access, the right to return to the Mansion for a second tour in the same day, and a Keepsake Backstage Pass. What this double-priced ticket does

FIG. 75

offer, however, is what every true Elvis pilgrim clearly yearns for: the feeling of being special, of being part of the King's entourage, of being a Very Important Elvis Person—in effect, of being admitted into the presence, albeit postmortem, of the King of Rock 'n' Roll. These same aspiring Elvis VIPs are likely to pay extra to be designated "Elvis Insiders," and they will probably strive to be elected president of their local fan club so that they, too, can gain access to special gatherings with access to special Elvis people.

While there are designated times year-round—morning Walk Ups and evening Walk Ups—when fans can make their way up to the Meditation Garden

FIG. 76

unescorted and at their own pace, the vast majority of both tourists and pilgrims get onto the grounds of Graceland proper in small buses that seat 16, at a rate of roughly 12 per hour, from 9 to 5 in the high season and 10 to 4 from November through February. They cross Elvis Presley Boulevard in rhythm with a synchronized traffic light and glide through Music Gates, which open just long enough to let a single bus through. But before boarding the bus, everyone in line is photographed in front of a Music Gates backdrop (fig. 76), whether they want to or not, and that print is available for purchase after the tour.

Certainly, the access fees are steep and the wait in line can be long, but an Elvis pilgrim would no sooner question his investment in his Graceland visit than would a pilgrim to Jerusalem question the cost and effort involved in getting to the Church of the Holy Sepulchre. This does not mean, however, that a Greek Orthodox pilgrim to Jerusalem will not have issues with what the Catholics are doing in and to their portion of that sacred site, or that the Armenians will not quarrel with the Copts, despite their shared beliefs. And all of them will certainly have issues with the local Israeli officials and with the Moslem community that has traditionally held the keys to the great door of the church. Similarly, Elvis pilgrims will passionately defend Graceland to cynical outsiders, and especially to the media, but at the same time they will freely complain about Elvis Presley Enterprises, Inc.—how the tours are managed, which rooms are open and which are not, and what is said by whom on the audio tour—and they will almost certainly have something disparaging to say about Priscilla, who, in their opinion, not only betrayed Elvis, but also redecorated Graceland "Hollywood style" (i.e., blue and white, instead of red).

Once through the wrought-iron door of the Mansion, after some general words outside from a guide and the donning of the audio headset, an alert first-time visitor may notice with some surprise that the small table clock just to the right of the entrance is stopped at 3:15 (fig. 77), which is approximately the time when Elvis was pronounced dead at Baptist Memorial Hospital in downtown Memphis, on the afternoon of August 16, 1977. The message is clear: from that moment forward, Graceland has been frozen in time. Just next to that stopped clock is a tall green canister that with some inspection reveals its contents to be emergency oxygen, a necessary first aid for those occasional pilgrims who faint when they enter the sacred Elvis home. This is the Elvis/Graceland version of the so-called Stenhdal syndrome, named for the 19th-century French novelist who described the dizzying,

FIG. 77

FIG. 78
FIG. 79

disorienting effect of a tourist's first face-to-face encounter with a famous work of art in Florence that he had for years longed to see in person; its counterpart phenomenon among Christian pilgrims to the Holy Land nowadays is the Jerusalem syndrome.

Mansion visitors encounter, in sequence, Elvis's living room, with its 17-foot white sofa and peacock stained glass room dividers setting off the small music room beyond (fig. 78); his glittering dining room, with its glass-covered dinner table beneath an elaborate chandelier fully set for six; his '70s-era kitchen, with its burnt-yellow refrigerator and electric range with (sometimes) plastic cherry pie (fig. 79); and Gladys' nearly all-white bedroom, with its deep purple bedspread and open closet with her dresses and purse. They then descend in tight gridlock down an enclosed, mirror-lined staircase to the lower level of the Mansion, there to see Elvis's yellow and black den with its three televisions (fig. 80) and his intimate fabric-lined pool room. Down the narrow hall leading to the stairs back up to the Mansion's main level is a small painting of a harbor with a clock tower whose tiny (real) clock is stopped at 25 minutes after three.

Visitors leave the Mansion by the back door, after coming upstairs from the den and pool room and strolling past the Jungle Room (fig. 81)—so named for its abundance of (faux) fur-covered furniture—and, if they are so inclined (and EPE security personnel are looking the other way), stroking its avocado shag wall covering. Out back, just beyond whatever audacious motor vehicle may be parked in the breezeway, there are two important audio stops before entering the Trophy Building, the low, barn-like extension on the Mansion's south wing. First, there is Vernon Presley's office, still looking as it did on March 8, 1960, when Elvis held his press conference

upon retuning from the Army, a video
of which is broadcast continuously on
a vintage TV. Just beyond, toward the
south, is Graceland Farm's original
pump house, which Vernon turned
into a smoke house and Elvis briefly
made into a private firing range which,
because of its small size, could only
have been useful for simulated pistol
combat at close quarters. Ultimately,
Elvis's firing range became a storage
shed, and it still houses a cobweb-
bound white Sears outboard motor.

FIG. 80
FIG. 81

Next, visitors enter the Trophy
Building, which was built on the
footprint of Graceland's original stone
patio. Here, both tourists and pilgrims
will be dazzled by a panoply of Elvis relics, beginning with his gold lamé suit and
white bucks of the '50s, complemented by a plethora of fan merchandise of the
period, including a Howdy Doody-like Elvis puppet. This is followed by scores of
gold and platinum records in the Hall of Gold (fig. 82), then a multitude of tes-
timonies to Elvis's philanthropy, including rows of cancelled checks and, finally,
costumes and paraphernalia from Elvis's movie years, as well as from his wedding to
Priscilla Beaulieu on May 1, 1967, from his *'68 Comeback Special*, and from his early
Vegas years.

Visitors then exit into the bright sunlight in the direction of the Meditation
Garden but are re-directed back to the Racket Ball Court just south of the storage
shed. This was initially the micro *locus sanctus* where Elvis was said to have sung his
last song, *Blue Eyes Crying in the Rain,* to girlfriend Ginger Alden in the wee hours of
the morning of August 16, 1977, before retiring with the first of what would ultimately be three regimens of drugs. More recently, though, the Racket Ball Court has
become the overflow space for Elvis's ever-growing collection of postmortem gold

FIG. 82

records, and more and more jumpsuits from his later Vegas years. Its highlight is the *Elvis—Aloha from Hawaii* costume from 1973, with a double eagle on its enormous belt clasp, displayed beneath a TV monitor with a continuously-running video of the concert.

Casual visitors may see Graceland through very different eyes. Many will form their opinion of the Mansion from the perspective of today—as a home fitting (or not) for the greatest entertainer of all time—while others will judge it in relationship to the Presley's meager early life in Tupelo. The former group, even before seeing the Hall of Gold in the Trophy Building with its hundreds of gold and platinum records, will struggle to reconcile this modest house in this run-down neighborhood with the King of Rock 'n' Roll, forgetting that Elvis bought Graceland when he was just 22 years old and chose to keep it as his home until the day he died.

Graceland will make much more sense—and have much greater impact—for the Tupelo group, especially after a visit to the Elvis Birthplace Complex. That 1939 Plymouth out back of Vernon's shotgun shack, pointing toward Memphis and signaling, according to the inscribed granite block nearby, the Presley family's 1948 departure in search of a better living, becomes a Cadillac just a decade later at Graceland. Similarly, that tiny wooden table in the birth house, just a few feet from the Presley pot belly stove, has become in Graceland Mansion a grand dining room table beneath a huge chandelier, adjacent to a large, modern kitchen. The family that slept together in a single bed in the front room in Tupelo would have the luxury at Graceland of multiple bedrooms, with the one for Elvis's beloved mother Gladys on the ground floor larger than Vernon's entire shotgun shack. And the list goes on, from Graceland's white, gold, and blue living room, to its music room just beyond with its stained-glass peacocks and its (sometimes) gold piano, to its downstairs yellow and black den with its three vintage TVs (ABC, CBS, and NBC, just like President Johnson), to its intensely cozy fabric-lined pool room with its tip-less pool cues, and finally, to its triumph-of-tacky Jungle Room upstairs. The transformation of Tupelo into Graceland is the transformation of America from the '40s to the '50s, with Elvis as its hero and Rock 'n' Roll as its enabling vehicle.

The Presley stables and an occasional horse grazing at the back of Graceland's grounds provide only passing distraction for the hordes of tourists and pilgrims that then line up to view Elvis's grave marker and associated votives (fig. 83), the last major stop before boarding the bus for the brief ride back to Graceland Plaza. Votives piled high by adoring fans sometimes cover the marker's thoroughly religions epitaph, written by Janelle McComb, poet and long-time friend of the Presleys, at the request of Vernon Presley. It identifies Elvis as "a precious gift from God," as someone with "a God-given talent that he shared with the world," and con-cludes, just above Elvis's TCB logo with:

> God saw that he needed some rest and
> called him home to be with Him,
> We miss you son and daddy. I thank God
> that He gave us you as our son.

Elvis's bronze grave marker is flanked to the left by that of Grandmother Minnie Mae Presley, who passed away in 1980, and to the right by the marker of father Vernon, who died in 1979. Just beyond Vernon's marker to the right is that of mother Gladys, who died at the age of 43 in August 1958, and there is even a small marker for Jesse Garon Presley, Elvis's still-born twin. This may all seem pretty straight-forward to the causal Graceland visitor, but Elvis *cognoscenti* know that Elvis was initially laid to rest in Forest Hills Cemetery, just off the freeway that leads north into downtown Memphis, and that his body and that of his mother

FIG. 83

Gladys—each enclosed in a heavy copper coffin—were transferred to Graceland's Meditation Garden on October 27, 1977, at Vernon's request and thanks to a special dispensation granted by city fathers that trumped the standing rule against back-yard burials. That came about because there was then high anxiety that Elvis's body would be stolen—and in fact, a bungled attempt to do just that took place only 11 days after the Forest Hills internment. The *cognoscenti* will also know that Jesse Garon was buried on January 9, 1935, in Priceville Cemetery just outside Tupelo, and that no body was ever found to transfer to Graceland since the Presleys could not then afford a marker. And they will also likely be fully aware that Elvis's middle name was spelled "Aron" and not, as the marker has it, "Aaron," and that the mix-up had much more to do with Vernon's limited education than with the theory propa-gated in the late '80s by Gail Brewer-Giorgio (*Is Elvis Alive?*) and perpetuated for years thereafter by Bill Beeny that this was a purposeful misspelling by Elvis him-self, who, still living, was superstitious enough to avoid a grave marker bearing his true name.

Once back across Elvis Presley Boulevard, perhaps with that expensive photo in hand taken an hour or so earlier in front of the Music Gates backdrop, those who opted for the Platinum or the Entourage VIP Tour will find a varied menu of addi-tional ticketed settings for experiencing the life and relics of Elvis. It will include the Automobile Museum, the Two Custom Airplanes, and several mini-museums embedded among the shops of Graceland Plaza and Graceland Crossing. There is the new (in 2009) Elvis in Hollywood Exhibit, with his personal scripts for some of his 31 movies, the new (in 2009) The King and Pop Culture Exhibit, where visitors can explore Elvis's impact on music and the world through a series of listening stations, the Private Presley Exhibit, and the '68 *Special* Exhibit, that includes the leather wristband Elvis wore during the filming.

Communitas

The appearance of the Elvis grave shrine in mid-August and the quality and tempo of activity around it are very different from the non-holiday season. During Elvis Week there will likely be more than 25,000 visitors to Graceland, and one senses immediately that as a group they stand apart; these make up the most concentrated pool of Elvis pilgrims and these, disproportionately, account for Elvis pilgrimage activity. Characteristically, the August Graceland pilgrim travels a greater distance than the June Graceland tourist and expends greater effort; almost certainly this will not have been the first visit. Paradigmatic, though extreme, is Pete Ball, the EP-tattooed London laborer who between 1982 and 1987 came to Graceland 53 times, all the while never stopping anywhere else in the United States. As a group, August pilgrims tend to be older than June tourists and they appear to be less affluent. These are the folks of America's blue-collar, working-class cities, especially of the Old South. (A survey of the license plates in the various Graceland parking lots bears this out.) August Elvis pilgrims were poetically evoked on site by Selby Townsend on the August 14, 1987 *Nightline* segment entitled Remembering Elvis, as "those very special people" who:

> *tease their hair, chew gum, swear, drink Pepsi Cola, smoke cigarettes, and dress too young for their years. They come here in Chevies and Fords…. Most of them went to high school and some even finished. And they all know what it's like to work for a living.*
>
> *We are the blue-collar workers, the fans, the believers in magic and fairytales. We're not smart enough not to fall in love with someone we never met. We're not rich enough to buy everything we want from the souvenir shops. We don't even have sense enough to come in out of the rain. But Lord, we've got something special.*
>
> *Only one that feels it can understand it. We share the sweetness, the emptiness, the understanding. We're the Elvis generation—wax fruit on our kitchen table, Brand X in our cabinet, a mortgage on our home, Maybelline on our eyes, and love in our hearts that cannot be explained or rained out. He was one of us.*

Nothing could be more unlike the anonymity and dispassion of tourist travel than the intense bonding that takes place among the faithful during Elvis Week. Anthropologists speak of the *communitas* ("commonness of feeling") of pilgrimage and emphasize the liminoid ("threshold") nature of the experience that, like a rite of passage, takes the pilgrim out of the flow of his or her day-to-day existence and leaves him or her in some measure transformed. Nowhere was community and bonding more apparent during the late '80s than at the Days Inn Motel on Brooks Road, between Graceland and the airport, the home of the Tribute Week Elvis Window Decorating Contest. *Communitas* began in the parking lot with its rows of Lincolns and Cadillacs bearing Elvis vanity plates, and it continued around the pool, where pilgrims gathered to drink Budweiser and reminisce. One sensed in the pool-side conversation of those days the inevitable evolution of recalled anecdote from, among the older fans, those stories relating to the living Elvis to, among the younger fans, those stories relating to extraordinary events surrounding postmortem August gatherings. This, too, must have had its counterpart in the early Christian world, as those pilgrims and locals with memories of the living saint died off; in the later 5th century, the distinction would have been between those who actually knew Simeon and those who knew only his empty column and his *vita*.

Although the texture of conversation then at the Days Inn was interwoven with accounts of the seemingly supernatural—the seeds of future Elvis miracles—its center of gravity was shifting toward stories of extraordinary pilgrimage, typically involving long distance and great sacrifice. There at poolside in 1989 was Betty Lou Watts (fig. 84), who had made the *Baltimore Sun* a year earlier for her extraordinary Elvis devotion and her collection of Elvis relics that included a pair of Elvis's black silk pajamas she claimed never to have worn. Betty Lou cheerily told anyone within earshot at poolside that she had never missed an Elvis Week since its inception in 1978, but that this year had been different. It seems that Betty Lou's son was at that very moment in a Baltimore hospital as the result of a bar fight—having been, as they say in cities like Baltimore, hit "up side the head" with a 2 x 4. With no extra cash, Graceland in mid-August was out of the question, until some of Betty Lou's local Elvis friends took up a collection and put her on the Greyhound Bus to Memphis. For those

FIG. 84

FIG. 85

gathered at the Days Inn that year, Betty Lou Watts was offering the stuff of *communitas*: a gratifying Elvis story with a gratifying Elvis outcome, worthy of the compassion and philanthropy that was the hallmark of Elvis himself.

Twenty years later, in 2009, EP vanity-plate Cadillacs were replaced by EP vanity-plate GMCs (fig. 85), African-American Elvis pilgrims were still in very short supply, and the hub of Elvis Week *communitas* shifted from the window decorating contest, which became much smaller, and at a Days Inn Motel just south of Graceland's Automobile Museum, to the Elvis Week Entertainment Tent in Graceland Crossing (fig. 86). (The Days Inn of the '80s has since gone into precipitous decline.) There, each day of Elvis Week, beginning at 12 noon, is an open microphone with a full menu of EP back-up music for aspiring Elvis tribute artists. Pilgrims stay for hours in and around the tent, making friends and swapping stories, just as in the past, and taking pictures of one another, against the musical backdrop of amateur Elvises whose singing skills range from the near sublime to the profoundly ridiculous. Budweiser is readily available from a nearby stand and there are plenty of Elvises in attendance (and a few Priscillas, too), who are there not to sing but simply to be seen. Some among the Elvises could be the King's contemporaries (fig. 87), and there are those at least as young as a little Tupelo Elvis, about five. The first up on August 13, 2009, was Danny Frazer, a paraplegic from birth. Despite his physical challenges, Danny gave a superb performance, but his impact on the fans was all the greater for having

FIG. 86

FIG. 87

no legs, especially when he sang *Walk a Mile in My Shoes*, tapping out the rhythm with his right hand (fig. 89). Cheers and tears erupted throughout the tent, there was the ritual passing of sweat scarves to 70-somethings in the front row and after 40 minutes, Danny Frazer was gone—though only after posing for photographs with a teen in a wheelchair. Like Betty Lou Watts 20 years earlier, Danny Frazer was creating Elvis Week *communitas* and, for some, a moment of liminality.

Much like Jerusalem pilgrims, Graceland pilgrims, whether at the Days Inn poolside in the late '80s or in the Entertainment Tent two decades later, acknowledge group identity not only through their license plates, but also through their clothing, jewelry, and tattoos (fig. 90). There is first-name familiarity among the "we" and an openness to new members, who are initiated through friendly interrogation: "How many times have you been to Graceland?" "How many Elvis concerts did you attend?" Elvis's motto in life was Taking Care of Business and the unspoken motto among the postmortem "we" is Taking Care of Elvis. The despised "other" extends well beyond the old familiar circle of Colonel Parker, Albert Goldman, and Memphis Mafia turncoat Lamar ("Lardass") Fike, who was Goldman's main inside source, to include Geraldo and the media in general, which is universally viewed among the fans as having always treated Elvis, his family, and his fans as southern

FIG. 89

hicks. Priscilla is in this evil mix as well, since her infidelity is believed by most to have destroyed Elvis's will to live and because she is generally acknowledged as having been "uppity" and as having wrecked Graceland by redecorating it.

From Priscilla the trail of suspicion and resentment extends to include Elvis Presley Enterprises, Inc. (the Estate), which she headed until recently, and especially its long-standing executive director, Jack Soden. Over the years, the Estate has been viewed more as a hindrance than a help to Elvis Week and Elvis fans, who know the truth; namely, that they (the fans) are the ones who created and sustain Elvis Week, despite the best efforts of those profit-driven, litigious folks in the head office to drain it of its true spirit. Stories abound among the Elvis faithful of EPE lawyers tracking down and bringing legal action against poor, good-hearted craftspeople who make the mistake of using Elvis images under copyright to make their cheap souvenirs. The Estate's most recent crime, though, was failing to send a forceful Elvis advocate (i.e., not Priscilla) to appear on *Larry King Live* in the days after Michael Jackson's death, to refute once and for all the misbegotten notion that Michael Jackson was bigger in life and will be bigger in death than Elvis. The confused and misguided are inclined to say that when Elvis died, "America cried," whereas when Michael Jackson died, "the whole world cried." Just hearing those detested words instantaneously adds a dose of heightened intensity to the *communitas* of August Graceland pilgrims.

A first-time visitor to Graceland during Elvis Week may be surprised by an aspect of its *communtas* that might otherwise be expected at Lourdes, Chimayo, and the Shrine of Brother André; namely, the number of sick and infirm in attendance, despite the stifling heat and humidity of

FIG. 90

August, despite the fact that Graceland Mansion is inaccessible to wheelchairs, and despite the steep path up to the Meditation Garden that must be ascended during the morning and evening Walk Ups to graveside. There is the bald husband and brother among a party of two otherwise robust couples in their 40s: a shrunken, frightened shell of a man swimming inside overlarge clothing, he is clearly undergoing chemotherapy and is now (one assumes) realizing a life-long dream. There is the Englishman of similar

FIG. 91

age dragging his all but inert lower body across Graceland Crossing with crutches, one slow, painful step after the other, as he quietly sings along to *Can't Help Falling in Love* (fig. 91). There is the paraplegic tribute artist Danny Frazer, the teenage girl beside the stage with whom he is photographed after his routine, and then there is 25-year-old "David," from Arkansas (fig. 92).

David, who had fallen asleep on a bench in the hot early-morning Memphis sun, was one of only a handful of fans lingering in Graceland Plaza at 8 am on August 16, 2009, from among the thousands who had gathered there the night before for the Candlelight Vigil and Walk Up, that ended at 4 am. David's black Elvis jumpsuit was stained with candle drippings and his feet were twisted inward so the toes of his shoes touched. David woke up to tell the (liminal) story of his transformation into a true Elvis believer a quarter century after the King's death. It seems that David's Memphis granddad had created a poster for Elvis early on, that his mom was a fan and kept all the clippings from August 16, 1977, and that David had started reading those clippings at age five. These readings, accompanied by Elvis music, drew him at age 18 to Memphis for the first of his seven consecutive Elvis Week pilgrimages, and it was then that it

FIG. 92

FIG. 93

happened. David proudly confesses that his first visit to the Mansion precipitated his "conversion," and that he is now passing his Elvis devotion on to his 3-year-old nephew. A similar moment of liminality can be imputed to the perpetually sad "June," from Oklahoma, at least to judge from her message on the Fans' Memorial Wall (fig. 93). After her conversion, "close to you [Elvis]," on August 13, 1995, June was moved to make 21 pilgrimages to Graceland in the next 14 years, including three trips in the year 2004 alone.

Larry Geller knows what this is all about, as does Maryanne Cox, Elvis's private nurse, who did a spot on Sirius Satellite Radio during Elvis Week 2009 with Memphis Mafia's eternally-youthful radio man George Klein. Maryanne remarked on the truism that Graceland at this time of year is a destination for "people in wheel-chairs and mothers with babies." But she retreated from fully embracing the *locus sanctus* implications of this observation with the half-hearted disclaimer that they come "not to pray but to celebrate a life." This same unstated awareness of, and dis-comfort with, the powerfully religious flavor of Elvis Week emerged as well in Linda Thompson's Sirius interview that same day. Linda, Elvis's big love after his divorce, discounted the notion of Elvis miracles, but then, incongruously, went on to recall that when little Lisa Marie called to say her daddy had died, the electricity in Linda's Los Angeles apartment went out—and hers was the only apartment in the block to loose electricity that day. These stories have meaning, and are repeated year after year, precisely because they are at once the stuff of faith and the glue of *communitas*.

Mimesis

Early Christian pilgrims sometimes gained the blessing of the holy place through *mimesis* ("imitation")—action imitative of the local sacred hero or event (Frazer's magical thinking: "the law of similarity"). This might involve simple imitative gestures at appropriate places and times, such as throwing stones at the grave of Goliath or lifting one of the surviving water-to-wine jugs at Cana "to gain a blessing," as the Piacenza Pilgrim did. Or it might entail a more subtle, ongoing identification with a particularly appropriate sacred figure whose story was believed to provide a model outcome from which the pilgrim might benefit. This is why many pilgrims sought burial close to the Cave of the Seven Sleepers, on the west coast of Turkey, near Ephesus: so that pilgrims could identify with and benefit from the sleepers' miraculous resurrection in the 5th century, after having been sealed up there in the cave, "asleep," for 200 years. What beliefs underlie sacred *mimesis*? On the level of the theology of the early Christian period, there was the general belief that the faithful should model their behavior on biblical figures and saints. Saint Basil, writing in the later 4th century, lays it our clearly:

> [In the scriptures] the lives of saintly men, recorded and handed down to
> us, lie before us like living images of God's government, for our imitation
> of their good works. … The lover of chastity constantly peruses the story
> of [the Patriarch] Joseph, and from him learns what chaste conduct is….
> Fortitude he learns from Job….

On a more basic level, though, there is the primal belief in "sympathetic magic," as it may be seen to operate at that period on gem amulets and among magical texts, called magical papyri because they are usually written on papyrus. Back pain was a major problem and a diagnostic puzzle then, just as it is now. The imagery common on gem amulets for back pain shows a field worker bending over to cut grain. Some among these amulets bear the word "sciatica" since their purpose was to render those carrying them immune from back pain, just as the laborer is immune. Among magical papyri this protective power is invoked through the Greek *hos...houto* formula: "as such and such happens (or not) to X, so also may such and such happen (or not) to me." Thus, as the laborer comfortably bends his back so also may I; as the Seven Sleepers miraculously rose from the dead and walked out of their cave/grave, so also may I. This is sometimes called the magic of persuasive analogy. It reflects the ageless belief that the assumption of identity brought with it a corresponding assumption of the protection, power or healing associated with the model. The 6th-century physician Alexander of Tralles prescribed for his patients with peptic stomach who could not keep their food down an amulet showing Herakles choking back the breath of the Nemean lion. Similarly, "our Mother Sarah," wife of the Patriarch Abraham, miraculously became pregnant with Isaac at age 90 and so she—her name and/or image—became an amulet for women trying to become pregnant.

Like Elvis, Simeon had imitators—in his case, those who replicated his column-dwelling asceticism at various times and in various places over more than a millennium. The most famous, who died on his column near Antioch in 592, not far from Simeon's vacant column, even took Simeon's name; he is now referred to as Saint Simeon the Younger, which means that the original Simeon is the Elder. Given that Simeon the Elder's column was a pilgrimage destination of even greater significance once vacant, after the saint's death, than during his lifetime, the appearance not far away, about a century later, of a new, living column-dwelling Simeon must have been greeted with great enthusiasm. After all, the audience was primed on how to react to and what to expect, in terms of good advice and miraculous healings, from a hair-shirted hermit standing on a tall column. Like his model of the 5th century, this 6th-century Simeon performed miracles with the aid of the dirt from around the base of his column. Blessed dirt is rubbed on the body of a paralytic so that he might walk, blessed dirt is "drunk" by a man with a bleeding ulcer in order that he might eat, and blessed dirt mixed with water is thrown on the deck of a pilgrim's ship foundering in high seas and the seas are calmed. And like his

FIG. 94

elder model, this younger Simeon received votives in thanks for his miracles, some of which show the saint at the top of his column and the recipient of the miracle below, and some of which show the healed body part, much like the contemporary votives affixed to the statue of Juan Diego at Guadalupe.

Sacred *mimesis*—in this case, the identification of the faithful, through their actions, with Christ in his Passion—is most fully realized at Chimayo in the biblical theatre that takes place just behind the chapel every year on Thursday afternoon before Good Friday. Members of the local parish take parts in a dramatic reenactment of the Passion, beginning with the Kiss of Judas, continuing through the Mocking of Christ (fig. 94) and the Crucifixion, and ending with the Lamentation of the Marys. Although the "blood" of this Passion play comes out of a can, feelings are intense, as each of the lay actors penetrates to the spiritual as well as to the historical core of his or her part.

Elvis *mimesis* is rampant at Graceland in mid-August and it is present there on some level all year around. It begins with the Elvis look-alikes, which in August number in the hundreds, and they come from all over the world. For some of these *ersatz* Elvises, this is their main identity and, if they can sing, maybe their day job as well, whereas for others, it is little more than a passing costume party. In the former category is Artie "Elvis" Mentz, two-time Oprah guest who, according to his website, was once honored by *Rolling Stone Magazine* as one of the five best Elvis Impersonators (as they used to be called) and now markets his Elvis charisma-approximating talents out of Dubuque, Iowa, with an oldies group called Artie & The Pink Cadillacs. Artie, who since age 12 has answered to "Elvis," figures prominently in the 1984 video *Mondo Elvis: The Strange Rites & Rituals of the King's Most Devoted Disciples,* in which he equates his relationship to the King to that of a priest to God, since both are filling in for "someone not there in body."

In the latter, "costume party" category, comprising August Elvises who return to a normal life, is Tord Johannson from Sweden. Tord appeared on stage behind Shoneys on Elvis Presley Boulevard during Elvis Week 1989, lip-syncing Elvis hits as George Klein broadcast live on 56-WHBQ and autographed photographs. It was obvious to the small crowd assembled there that Tord was not a gifted singer and that he could barely keep the beat; moreover, his jet black hair was rapidly giving up its temporary color in rivulets of black sweat streaming down his face. But it all ended well: 20 years later, Professor Tord Johannson, middle-aged and balding, could be found pursuing his career in experimental physics at Sweden's prestigious Uppsala University—and yes, according to his Facebook page, Tord is still an avid Elvis fan.

Depending on how close the facial and body match is to Elvis—either to the gold lamé rocker of the '50s or the jump-suited crooner of the '70s—the mere presence among Elvis fans of someone whose hairstyle, clothing, gestures, and voice evoke the King creates the potential for a charismatic moment. Moreover, like the Passion players and their spectators behind the chapel at Chimayo on Holy Thursday, everyone at Graceland during Elvis Week knows how to perform his or her part, and the resulting theatre and associated evoked charisma at once reinforce *communitas* and invite liminal experiences. Then add to that already potent mix Elvis singing and gyrating, and the result is magical, if not miraculous. During Elvis Week, the *gestalt* of Overton Park in 1954 and of the International Hotel in Las Vegas in 1971 are recaptured over and over again each day in the tent at Graceland Crossing and (in 2009) during the evenings of August 12th and 13th at The Orpheum, in downtown Memphis, during the Ultimate Elvis Tribute Artist Contest.

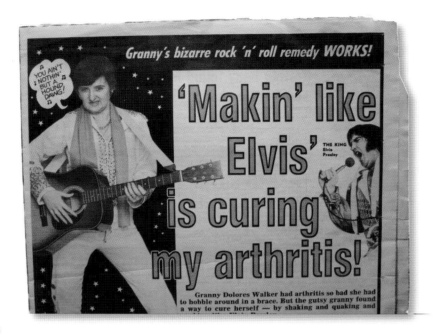

FIG. 95

(Unlike the tent, the downtown event is an expensive extravaganza orchestrated by the Estate, and therefore subject to much criticism.) For those in attendance who had direct experience of Elvis during his lifetime, these imitation Elvises reinforce a truth and re-confirm and re-energize a powerful emotional feeling, whereas for Elvis neophytes, they offer a point of entry to liminality.

One does not have to accept the claim in the *Weekly World News* of October 2, 1990, that a certain grandmother named Dorlores Walker got rid of her arthritis (think sciatica) by gyrating like Elvis (fig. 95) to believe in the potential therapeutic value of Elvis *mimesis* among the faithful. According to the article, Dolores, who had been a fan since age 13:

> had arthritis so bad she had to hobble around in a brace. But the gutsy
> granny found a way to cure herself—by shaking and quaking and mak-
> ing like Elvis Presley.

Even discounting such doubtful tabloid testimony, there is much anecdotal evidence to consider, including the wheelchair bound Elvis look-alike David, from Arkansas, who becomes Elvis each year in August, likely as some form of personal therapy, as well as the paraplegic tribute artist Danny Frazer and the wheelchair-bound girl with whom he was photographed at stage-side in the tent.

FIG. 96

And there is the testimony of Dr. Jukka Ammondt from Finland, who for years taught literature at Jyväskylä University and, late in life, sought out Elvis, through *mimesis*, in a time of intense emotional stress. Jukka showed up at the second and last International Conference on Elvis Presley, titled Elvis and the Sacred South, organized by Vernon Chadwick at the University of Mississippi in early August 1996. (The Conference's termination after convening #2 may have had something to do with the Chancellor's reaction to an evening's entertainment that featured Elvis Herselvis and the Straight White Males, from San Francisco.) The story Jukka Ammondt told at the conference was at once simple, odd, and affecting. It seems that he and his wife of many years had gone though a painful divorce and he was spiritually adrift. So Jukka decided to combine three life interests as a therapeutic diversion: his love of Latin (which is common in Finland), his love of Elvis, and his love of singing. He translated Elvis hits into Latin, sang them to anyone who would listen, recorded them, and then brought them, via high-tech lip-sync, to the stage of the Yerby Conference Center auditorium in Oxford, Mississippi, during a brutal summer heat wave, and set up a table afterwards to sell his CD (fig. 96). Happily, Jukka Ammondt was by then feeling much better.

Elvis look-alikes and tribute artists are hardly confined to Graceland and mid-August. They can be secured quickly almost anywhere via the internet for birthday parties or other special occasions, they are the featured entertainment on Caribbean winter cruises, and they are fixtures in second-tier venues along the Strip in Las Vegas. Worldwide, one does not have to go far to find an Elvis look-alike ready to sing. In Israel, there is an Elvis "guild"—reputedly confined to Elvises from among the Sephardic Jewish community, to the exclusion of the Ashkenazi—ready to supply an Elvis or two appropriate for any occasion. One among them, who in the '90s claimed to be the only true "Israeli Elvis" because he alone among the guild members had actually been to Graceland, was the model for a large fiberglass statue of the King outside the Elvis Inn (and gas station) at Abu Gosh, on the road from Tel Aviv to Jerusalem (fig. 97).

Blue-collar Baltimore, just south of the Mason-Dixon Line, has a wildly-popular Elvis event that takes place each year on the first weekend in December at the Lithuanian Hall, not far from the home of H. L. Mencken. Called the Night of 100 ELVISes, it has been a growing phenomenon since its first incarnation in 1994 and now, by popular demand, it extends over two nights and always sells out. Moreover, it currently attracts many more than the advertised 100 Elvises, some of whom arrive with a Priscilla. Doors open at 6:30 pm and close at 2:00 am, and, given the neighborhood, many attendees choose to shuttle in from area hotels. For this event, the otherwise staid Lithuanian Hall is transformed into an Elvis Ballroom, an Elvis Lounge (downstairs), and a Jungle Room (upstairs). The basic ticket is $55 (2010), which is nearly double that of Graceland's basic Mansion Tour, but that ticket brings with it a complementary southern buffet with Elvis food (meatloaf and mashed potatoes) and free drinks, including Lithuanian beer. And, like Vegas, there are stage-side tables in the Elvis Lounge available for local VIPs at inflated prices. The spirit and at least some of the players of the Graceland tent of August are reprised in Baltimore's Lithuanian Town Hall in December and, with them, a huge dose of Elvis *communitas* and Elvis charisma.

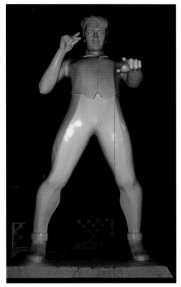

FIG. 97

Even if you don't sing like Elvis, or look or even dress like Elvis, you can *be* like Elvis at Graceland, year around, for a price. Elvis *mimetic* consumer opportunities begin with check-in at Elvis Presley's Heartbreak Hotel, conveniently located across the street from Graceland Mansion. Regular rooms, which look remarkably like Gladys's bedroom in the Mansion, have Elvis photographs on the wall as well as an Elvis movie channel and Elvis radio available day and night. But for a little extra cash, one can stay in an Elvis-themed suite, in "full Elvis style" (for $549 in 2010, but suites sleep up to eight). Each themed suite celebrates a different phase in Elvis's career:

> *The Burning Love Suite features a rich, romantic décor (lots of red). It is inspired by Elvis's 1972 hit record Burning Love and his status as a romantic idol.*

FIG. 98

Imagine stepping out for the first time onto the sidewalks of Graceland Plaza from your themed Elvis suite in the Heartbreak Hotel during Elvis Week. Opportunities abound among the many EPE vendors for being like and doing like Elvis. In the Everything Elvis store, you and a friend can shoot pool for 30 minutes for $100, on the very table on which Elvis played pool with the Beatles the night of August 27, 1965, in his home in Bel Air, California (fig. 98). At the conclusion of the game, you will receive a Certificate of Authentication and a Polaroid photograph to document the occasion. Just a few feet away, priced at $3,300, is an Aloha Jumpsuit (fig. 99), closely modeled on the original in the Vegas costume display in Elvis's Racquetball Court behind the Mansion. Then, just beyond the '68 Special Shop, where you can buy your own copy of the leather outfit Elvis wore for that concert, is a bike shop called Graceland Harley-Davidson. There, you can contract for one of the last of the 30 EP Signature Series created in 2007 and modeled after Elvis's 1957 black FLH model, so that you can "ride with the King," Or, if its nearly $60,000 price tag is too steep, you can instead purchase a raffle ticket for the Harley to be given away at the culmination of Elvis Week. And sooner or later you will discover the pink Cadillac parked under the marquee for the Scottish Inn & Suites, just up

FIG. 99

Elvis Presley Boulevard (fig. 100); this can be had for its Blue Book price of $16,000, which by comparison with the motorcycle seems like a bargain. Hungry? Drop into Rockabilly's Diner and order up (for just $4.95) what is colloquially called an "Elvis," because he loved this particular food item so much (fig. 101). An "Elvis" is a peanut butter and banana sandwich on white bread, browned in butter. And if you should find this cheap and filling sandwich appealing, you can take home an EPE-approved Authentic Recipe on a Graceland postcard, with these easy instructions:

Peel and mash [two] bananas. Mix [one cup] peanut butter with bananas thoroughly. Toast [six slices of white] bread lightly and spread mix on bread. Melt [one stick] butter in skillet and brown sandwiches on each slowly until golden brown.

In a matter of just a few hours after waking from the bliss of having slept just like Elvis, you will be given the opportunity to shoot pool, dress in a jumpsuit, ride a Harley, and eat, all just like Elvis.

Rituals

In the early Christian period, the Latin word *peregrinatio* meant simply "going abroad," most typically "for the sake of prayer" at a sacred destination, and there "to venerate," which meant to touch and kiss the sacred object, and to bow one's forehead to the ground before it. From travel diaries like those of the Spanish noblewoman Egeria (ca. 380) and the pilgrim from Piacenza (ca. 570), we know that the early

FIG. 100

FIG. 101

Christian pilgrim's encounter with a *locus sanctus* typically included a Bible reading
appropriate to the location, preceded and followed by prayers, as well as individual
ritualized gestures, which often included some action imitative of the original
sanctifying event—like throwing rocks at Goliath's tomb in imitation of the rock-
slinging David. There were things for the pilgrim to take away that could range from
local fruit to a fragment of the local relic, such as a chip from Simeon's column, to
"blessings," which were (and still are) bits of dirt or drops of oil or water that have
come in contact with one or more of the local relics.

In those instances where the *locus sanctus* was made holy not by Christ
or some other biblical figure, but rather by a living or departed holy man, as at
Simeon's shrine, the sacred story could be imparted to pilgrims on site though
private or collective recitation of the saint's *vita*, and through contemplation of
on-site votives documenting specific miracles. And everywhere there was touching.
Paulinus of Nola, writing in the early 5th century, claimed that the main reason pilgrims went to Jerusalem was to "see and touch" the places where Christ had been.
Moreover, what was true among early Christian pilgrims is true among Jerusalem
pilgrims to this day. Not only do they kneel and pray before the Stone of Unction in
the Church of the Holy Sepulchre, they lean forward to touch it as well and, before

departing, they are likely to buy a plastic container with locally sanctified dirt or oil. Again, the magical thinking of contagion is at work: the primordial belief that the essence of a person or a thing can be transferred through touch to another person or thing and thereby permanently enhance it.

The behavioral profile of the August Graceland pilgrim will be very different from that of the June Graceland tourist. While the latter's essentially dispassionate experience will likely be restricted to a few hours and center on the Graceland Mansion tour, followed by a stroll through the shops of Graceland Plaza, the former group's experience will probably extend over several days and will be distinctly "bi-polar," both by location and by tone. One pole—that of *communitas*—will be at poolside at the Days Inn or in the tent at Graceland Crossing, and the other pole will be in the Meditation Garden, specifically at the Elvis grave. The former is a social experience whereas the latter is thoroughly private and devotional; the mood at poolside and in the tent is festive, whereas at graveside it is somber. The prime opportunity for private Elvis devotions during Elvis Week is the early morning Walk Up to the Meditation Garden. The mood is prayerful and empathetic, not so much between one visitor and another as between each individual and Elvis himself. Some among those gathered mimetically take on the persona of the tortured Elvis, as if they and the King become one at this solemn moment and hallowed location. All players are on some level animated by their shared recollection of Elvis's recording of the powerfully affective melody and words of C. Austin Miles's famous hymn *In the Garden.*

The hushed silence in the Mediation Garden during the Walk Up is occasionally broken by muffled sobbing. Moreover, much as pilgrims to Chimayo form a quiet, orderly line leading into the side chapel with its sacred sand pit, Graceland pilgrims process reverently toward that special location just in front of Elvis's grave. Behind them as they stand or kneel in devotion is a comforting statue of Jesus with open arms, and just beyond the Elvis grave marker is Elvis's Eternal Flame (to match those of John F. Kennedy and Martin Luther King, Jr.). There is sympathetic acceptance among those waiting their turn for the ritualized bowing, kneeling, and praying of the pilgrim who has reached that sacred destination (fig. 102). What are they silently saying as they bow their heads, as they kneel, and as they weep? Most

FIG. 102

likely, what is true of the spoken collective piety of the Candlelight Service is true as well of that special *sub voce* moment of individual piety at graveside. During that service, Christian words and concepts provide the context and set the tone, the Bible and Jesus are often referenced, and, of course, Elvis is constantly evoked. The Candlelight Service is a one-sided conversation, and likely the same holds true for the silent prayers at graveside. A clue to their tone and substance is provided by the extended prayer-poems to Elvis left by fans at graveside. "Patricia's" communication (2009), titled "Love," is accompanied by a fluffy white teddy bear. Like most, it is presented as a poem:

I cannot remember a day without you, a day when
your smile did not come in to my view, a day when
your eyes did not shine through.

No, I cannot imagine a day without you.

I cannot remember laughing without thinking of you,
when your uproarious laughter was never more-true,
when your contagious hilarity did not lift my blues.

No, I cannot imagine laughing without you.
I cannot remember a day without singing with you,
when our heavenly father did not sing with us to. [sic]
No, I cannot imagine singing without you.
I remember the day I cried for you. The day the world
tried to comprehend you. They may never
understand, but I do.
My happiest times were always with you.

Nearby, "Margaret," from New Orleans, concludes her extended graveside prayer-poem, titled "My Sweet Elvis!," with *communitas*-fueling sentiments that build on Patricia's "They may never understand, but I do" notion:

You were such a great man that gave all that he had,
That's why the media can make me so mad.
They don't know what to say, they don't know what to do,
They say so many things that are not even true.

They just can't figure out why we love you so,
but if you're not an Elvis fan, you will never know.
How wonderful you are and that you'll always be,
the King of Entertainment for all Eternity.

As for the almost overpowering desire to touch among Elvis pilgrims, this is evident in the frequency with which those at graveside lean forward to touch the brass marker, as well as by the ubiquitous "Don't Touch" signs on the grounds and in the Mansion, by the many strategically-placed stations, and, where these are inadequate, as at the point where visitors pass the Presley kitchen stove, by molded sheets of protective plastic.

Elvis fans collaborate with the Estate in a wide verity of ritualized group encounters not only during Elvis Week, but also, on a somewhat smaller scale, on the days surrounding Elvis's birthday, January 8. This an especially attractive time for a visit to Graceland, since Christmas decorations are still in place in and around the Mansion. Elvis's 75th Birthday Celebration in 2010 was an unusually elaborate version of that annual milestone, extending over four days. Highlights listed on the Graceland website began on January 7 with a day trip to Tupelo to explore the Elvis birth house, with an Elvis Traveling Trivia Contest along the way and, that evening, an official tour of the Mansion in all its holiday splendor for Elvis Insiders (which anyone can become for a fee of $19.99). There was Elvis Christmas music playing in the background and special Elvis exhibits from the Graceland archive displayed around the residence. Later, across the street in Graceland Plaza, there were passed *hors d'oeuvres* and cash bars, and the chance to meet, among others who knew Elvis personally, Robin Koon, his co-star in *Follow That Dream*. And finally, at 12:01 am, fans from across the globe gathered in the dining room of the Heartbreak Hotel to sing familiar gospel songs and, of course, *Happy Birthday* to Elvis.

Later that morning, everyone congregated in Graceland Plaza for the official proclamation of Elvis Presley Day and the cutting of Elvis's birthday cake, with ex-wife and daughter, Priscilla and Lisa Marie, and officials of Elvis Presley Enterprises doing the honors. There was much for fans to choose from later in the day, including the opportunity to meet Elvis's close friend and manager, George Klein, and purchase an autographed copy of his new book, *Elvis: My Best Man*. Then, for Elvis fans that like basketball, the match up that evening between the Memphis Grizzlies and the Utah Jazz was designated Elvis Birthday Night, and for those not so inclined, there was the Elvis Dance Party, where birthday pilgrims could "hang out and enjoy a private party with [their] fellow Elvis fans." Ongoing from January 6 through 8, fans gathered to play Bingo at various set times in the dining room of the Heartbreak Hotel. Elvis's 75th Birthday Celebration continued unabated on January 9, as Elvis fan club presidents got together in the morning at the Memphis Marriott to learn firsthand about what clubs around the world were doing "to continue Elvis's name and memory," and to meet Marilyn Mason, who co-starred with Elvis in the *Trouble with Girls*. That afternoon, Tupelo historian Roy Turner hosted Conversations on Elvis, an open exchange that focused on all things Presley and Tupelo; guests included Guy Harris, a lifelong friend of Elvis whose mother was best friends with Gladys. In the evening, fans could first enjoy the "Elvis 75th Birthday Bash on Beale [Street]" and then take in the Memphis Symphony Orchestra's performance of Elvis Birthday Pops, highlighting Elvis's best-loved tunes. Finally, on the morning of Sunday, January 10, in the ticket pavilion of Graceland Plaza, the Southern Gospel Celebration brought Elvis's 75th birthday party to a close in a manner appropriate to both the day and the time, and to the specifically Christian spirituality that unites Elvis with his fans.

In the late '80s, the living Elvis oral tradition was institutionalized during Elvis Week in the annual Humes High Symposium featuring, among others, Elvis's belt maker and horse trainer (Mike McGregor), drummer (D. J. Fontana), and cook (Nancy Rook), just as the Taking Care of Elvis tradition was institutionalized in the yearly Fan Appreciation Social at the Memphis Airport Hilton. In those days Elvis pilgrims were petitioning (successfully) for an Elvis stamp and (unsuccessfully) for an Elvis holiday, and then they would gather to grill the powers that be within the inner circle of Graceland on the present state of the Elvis "image." A report in a Baltimore fan newsletter of the period included the following characteristic exchange:

> *Mr. Soden was also questioned as to why Graceland was not responding to the 'Elvis is Alive' thing. His main reply was that Graceland did not want to fuel the publicity by replying and were hoping it would just go away. But it hasn't. Does Graceland have to dig up Elvis's body to prove that he died?*

There was at that same gathering a brief, angst-filled exchange about the then new colorization of some of Elvis's early black and white movies. It seems that Elvis's gray sweater in a certain scene from *Rip it Up* had been given the color green, and "everyone knows" that Elvis couldn't stand the color green. How could they have done that? Emotions ran high, and the universally acknowledged, often-repeated aim of this was to present the world with a positive image of Elvis—the real Elvis.

The two poles of the mid-August experience, social and devotional, merge in the group ritual that is the highlight of Elvis Week: the Annual Candlelight Vigil, Service, and Walk Up. By mid-afternoon on August 15, 2009, the most devoted fans have already staked out their spots along the sidewalk in front of the Fans' Memorial Wall with lawn chairs and often umbrellas as shields against the blistering

FIG. 103

sun (fig. 103); the temperature that day is 98 degrees and the humidity nearly as high. By 6 pm, with increasing numbers of fans falling in place along the three layers of stanchions stretching most of the way down the Wall, a paramedic truck from the Fire Department of Memphis has taken up its position across the street. Multiple police cars appear toward 7:30 to block off Elvis Presley Boulevard, and as they do, those several dozen ardent fans who have brought their own portable Elvis shrines swarm out to claim their territory in the street (fig. 104); they look remarkably like those devotees who filled Saint Peter's Square during the vigil in honor of John Paul II, just after he died. By 8 pm, the line of fans waiting for the Music Gates to open has spilled out beyond the stanchions into the street; the sun is by then behind the trees to the west, fans are lighting the votive candles that are part of their shrines, and an Israeli Elvis appears out of the crowd (fig. 105).

The formal Candlelight Service, which every year since the inception of the Vigil in 1978 has been led by the Elvis Country Fan Club of Austin, Texas, begins at 8:50. A public relations representative of the Estate appears first to speak, from a platform behind the Wall and just to the right of the Music Gates; he is mostly ignored by the crowd. The graveside eternal flame has by then been brought down from the Meditation Garden by several of the Austin fan club members and the

FIG. 104

lighting of the candles held by the fans in the street begins, and proceeds very
quickly, given that most light their candles with their own cigarette lighters (many
Elvis fans are smokers). (The candles and wax deflectors are supplied free by the
Estate across the Boulevard in Graceland Plaza.) Everyone dutifully holds up his
or her candle at the instruction of the EPE representative as bright television
lights pan the crowd; the intent, he says, is to show the world what is happening at
Graceland. Then, over strategically placed loudspeakers, Elvis breaks into *If I Can
Dream,* to which everyone sings along as they wave their candles from side to side;
by the time the familiar reference to candles in the third stanza is heard—"Out
there in the dark, there's a beckoning candle"—many in the crowd have begun to
weep (fig. 106).

The "service" *per se,* which lasts about 15 minutes, is conducted by five solemn
female members of the Elvis Country Fan Club, dressed in matching club T-shirts.
The gravity of the moment and the wonder of Elvis are the over-arching themes,
with the last of the speakers, who looks to be born after 1977, confessing proudly
in a voice on the verge of tears that: "I live only for you, Elvis." The emotion of the
moment is palpable, though the homiletic tone 20 years earlier had more squarely
focused on the idea of the fans' shared guilt. In 1989 the service was based on a

FIG. 105

popular song Elvis recorded, *Always on My Mind*, and it focused specifically on the issue of the fans' role in Elvis's martyrdom. Recited tearfully to a hushed crowd comparable in size to that gathered at the 2009 service, it included these revealing sentiments:

Looking back through the years as we take this moment to remember—I have regrets. I regret all of those little things that I should have said and done to let you know how much you mean to me, Elvis…. A thousand souls joined together in harmony, as we are tonight, can only hope to return some of the love that Elvis has shared with each and every one of us. Though we are united as one, we know that Elvis belongs to each and every one of us exclusively….

Elvis…left us all with a very special gift—the gift of his love. Elvis gave unselfishly of himself to all of us, but did we, his fans, give as much of ourselves to him?

FIG. 106

FIG. 107

The last of the five speakers in 2009 does what each of her predecessors has done since the first Candlelight Service in 1978: she calls for a minute of silence in memory of Elvis (fig. 107). The absolute silence of that solemn interlude is finally broken by Elvis, this time singing one of his less familiar but clearly appropriate gospel songs: *Jesus Knows Just What I Need*. The implication is clear to each person in the crowd: Jesus knows that I need Elvis, just like the last speaker, who "lives only for Elvis." At this point, just a few minutes after 9 pm, the crowd begins to shuffle in preparation for the Walk Up. Following a group-sing of *Can't Help Falling in Love* (of course, with Elvis), the song with which Elvis closed his concerts in later years, the Music Gates swing open and the candlelight procession begins to snake its way up the driveway to the Meditation Garden and the graveside. There is a powerful sense of group-enforced reverence and solemnity, which has just been mandated both by the representative of the Estate and by the Elvis Country Fan Club speakers. The last pilgrim will lay his or her votive on the bronze tomb slab around 4 am. Like nearly every aspect of Graceland during Elvis Week, the Candlelight Vigil has its counterpart in Christianity. The vigil or evening service before the commemoration day of a saint or an important biblical event has been part of *locus sanctus* pilgrimage ritual for 17 centuries, as has the link between flame and "imminent presence" at holy graveside. Its earliest and still most familiar manifestation is Holy Fire, the miraculous flame marking the Resurrection of Christ; in Orthodox Christianity it comes during Holy Week as the culmination of the Pascal Vigil, at the stroke of midnight between Holy Saturday and Easter Sunday, signifying the resurrection of Christ.

Sacred Souvenirs

Graceland, like all *loca sancta* from the earliest centuries of Christianity to the present day, is not only a place to see and touch relics, it is a place to acquire sacred souvenirs. There was lively traffic in Byzantium, beginning in the 4th century, for relics of all sorts. As a new city with virtually no important Christian figures in its past, the Byzantine capital of Constantinople was relic poor. For major relics, which meant virtually anything that was unique, like the True Cross or the right index finger of John the Baptist (the one with which he pointed out Jesus), there was tight control over ownership and movement, and that control usually rested with a major church, a city or even the Byzantine state itself. Such was the case with the head of the deacon Stephen, the first Christian martyr, who was stoned to death just outside the north gate of Jerusalem. When his head made its journey to Constantinople in 421 at the command of the Byzantine emperor Theodosius II and his wife Eudocia, a special church was built to house it. Moreover, the entire city turned out to celebrate the moment when the holy head, now enclosed in a small reliquary casket, made its way up the city's main street in the care of two bishops, atop a chariot pulled by a pair of mules.

Of course, the normal, everyday spectator along the parade route could never expect personally to own such a relic. Recall the story of the military escort for the body of Saint Simeon, which took place about 40 years later, in the summer of 459. The military was called into action to prevent Simeon pilgrims from stealing a patch of the hermit's hair shirt—or, much worse, a piece of his corpse. In fact, the one person who laid a hand on the saint's body—the Bishop of Antioch, who sought just a hair from his beard—found that hand instantly turning leprous. The reliquary with Simeon's bones was destined for the city of Antioch and later, when the Byzantine emperor in far-away Constantinople demanded the body for the empire's capital, he was rebuffed, since, as the inhabitants of Antioch knew all too well, they had no fortified walls to protect them like those shielding Constantinople; Simeon, in the form of his miracle-working bones was Antioch's trusted protector.

It was not for lack of trying that ordinary Christians of the period did not lay their hands on the really important, one-of-a-kind relics. Around 380 a wealthy Spanish pilgrim named Egeria recorded in her travel diary what she witnessed in the Church of the Holy Sepulchre. She describes the dramatic moment when the wood of the True Cross is taken out of its gold and silver box and placed on a table before the seated bishop. She notes that he rests his hands on the relic, holding it down as the deacons keep careful watch. Why the precautions? Because they fear that someone will steal a piece of the wood, as they come forward to bend over and kiss it. She continues: "On one occasion...one of them bit off a piece of the Holy Wood and stole it away."

In the absence of what are sometimes called primary relics, early pilgrims had to rely on what they called *eulogiai* or "blessings." For them, the word held special meaning, referring to the blessing received by contact with a holy person, holy place or holy object. This contact blessing could either be received directly and immaterially through action, as by kissing the wood of the True Cross or by reclining on the couch in the Garden of Gethsemane where Jesus had reclined, or it could be received indirectly and materially, through an object or substance which had itself been blessed and empowered by physical contact with (or even mere proximity to) the holy. This could be nearby earth or fruit, or a bit of stone chipped from a stylite's column. More typically, though, the pilgrim's material blessing was received by way of some common substance that had been purposefully brought into contact with the holy—usually earth, oil, wax, water or cloth.

By the 6th century, the pilgrim's menu of such blessings was varied; moreover, an experience initially dominated by seeing and hearing was becoming increasingly tactile and kinetic. The Piacenza pilgrim got most of his blessings in the direct action way. He tells us, for example, that he took a bath in the spring at Cana "to gain a blessing"; similarly, he took a dip in the Jordan River "to gain a blessing," and reclined on the couch in the Garden of Gethsemane "to gain a blessing." In each of these instances, the Piacenza pilgrim gained his blessing through action

and contact. In other cases, however, he describes a blessed object or substance that might be carried away. Two, oil and earth, are mentioned in his account of the Tomb of Christ. The oil is drawn from the bronze lamp that burns at the head of the slab where the body of Jesus had lain, while the earth is simply placed inside the Tomb and "those who go in take some as a blessing." Surprisingly, the pilgrim from Piacenza rarely gives any hint of why he wants these blessings or, for the take-away variety, what he intends to do with them. Others, however, are much more explicit, and leave no doubt that these little bits of sanctified matter were more than simple mementos. Cyril of Skythopolis (ca. 555) writes that Saint Sabas used oil of the True Cross to exorcise evil spirits, while a century earlier, Theodoret of Cyrrhus describes a man who, in order to repel the nocturnal visit of demons, attached to the head of his bed "[a] flask of oil of the martyrs, with a blessing gathered from very many martyrs." A comparable effect is attributed by Saint Augustine (d. 430) to holy earth from Jerusalem; he describes a friend who received some from Jerusalem as a gift and "this he had hung in his bedroom in case he, too, should suffer some harm from demons."

Both the year-around Graceland tourist and the August Graceland pilgrim will take things home from their visit, though their respective mix of objects will likely be different. There are the traditional sorts of tourist trinkets available in the many EPE shops across from Graceland Mansion, with the teddy bear ranking at the top (fig. 108). The point of reference is Elvis's early hit (*Let Me Be Your*) *Teddy Bear*; with such a purchase, each fan, casual or ardent, can easily have Elvis as his or (mostly) her own teddy bear—as "Carolynn" asserts through her message on the Fans' Memorial Wall: "Elvis, you are my Teddy Bear." Many August pilgrims will not even take their purchase home with them, but rather will turn around and deposit their new furry friend at graveside as a votive.

The shops of Graceland Plaza also offer, of course, T-shirts, hats, and coffee mugs that will affirm *communitas* both on site and back home. There are also stacks of Elvis books (fig. 109), with new insider accounts appearing each year with a strong propagandistic thread throughout, aiming to reveal the "real Elvis" to those, in August, who already know who the real Elvis is. For those Graceland visitors who want to feel special—an aspiration that characterizes Elvis Week pilgrims—there is a long menu of special Elvis items for sale in Graceland Plaza at higher prices, beyond the *mimesis*-inspired concert outfits and Harley-Davidsons already mentioned. A doll-house size version of the Jungle Room can be had for $49.98 and a fancy Limited Edition Elvis pen is nearly twice that, at $96; like the expensive and shiny "Love Me Tender" Elvis figurine nearby, the pen comes with a "certificate of authenticity." The highest level of Elvis-purchase distinction during Elvis Week belongs to those items created for discerning fans by special craftsmen and artists who have their scheduled time posted at the various Graceland Plaza shops. There is Lowell Hays, "Jeweler to the King," who can now be your jeweler as well, and there is Joe Petruccio, "Renowned Elvis Artist," who can create something Elvis uniquely for you and on the spot, for the right price (fig. 110).

FIG. 109

FIG. 110

Of course Graceland relics in the early Christian sense—parts of Elvis himself (his hair), objects that have been empowered and given value by virtue of contact with Elvis (a concert sweat scarf) or material Elvis may have been physically close to but perhaps never actually touched (Graceland dirt)—are another matter altogether. Elvis Presley Enterprises does its best to make sure that nothing that is a true Elvis relic is ever touched, including the floor in the Mansion, whose carpet has been pulled up and discarded many times since Graceland opened to the public in 1982.

Elsewhere on the Presley pilgrimage route, though, where others are in charge, the rules have traditionally been more relaxed. In Tupelo, at the Elvis shotgun shack equivalent of the Bethlehem manger, visitors freely touch the Elvis pot belly stove (probably not knowing it is a replacement) and at Humes Jr. High they were allowed to stroke the Elvis football uniform. As for taking away a true Graceland relic, or even a piece of one, this is all but impossible, thanks to the strict policing efforts of the Estate. Highly motivated Graceland pilgrims, though, have found their own solutions. It is clear in the basement pool room of the Mansion that Elvis pilgrims have not only been inappropriately touching things Elvis, they have been surreptitiously taking things Elvis away. This room is smaller and more intimate than any other on the tour, and therefore more difficult to guard. The tent card on the pool table with its admonition not to touch only confirms that touching has been taking place. Much more significant, though, is the evidence over one's left shoulder just inside the door. There on the wall is the Elvis cue rack with an assortment of Elvis pool cues, none of which, for obvious reasons, retains its felt tip.

FIG. 111

Anyone who has been introduced to the thriving trade in Elvis relics (scarves, shoes, shirts, hair) by way of e-Bay or Jerry Osborne's *Presleyana* series will likely be puzzled by the meager offerings in the shops of Graceland Plaza. One has to look long and hard to find an Elvis 45 in its original sleeve for sale or a Lucite paper weight with a plug of Graceland dirt authenticated by EPE's Director of Merchandising & Licensing embedded in its base. (Recall the readily available dirt both at Chimayo and at Jim Morrison's grave in Père-Lachaise Cemetery.) The days have long since passed when Elvis's high school chum (then Marine and then mail carrier on disability) Sid Mckinney would stroll Graceland Plaza hawking his 1953 Humes High yearbook with an Elvis inscription for $4,500 (fig. 111). In the days of roaming Sid McKinney, this aspect of Elvis Week was different. An active formal trade in what the fans call "Elvis stuff" then centered on the Annual Elvis Presley Benefit Auction at the Whitehaven United Methodist Church on Elvis Presley Boulevard, while informal trading in this material took place almost continuously on the sidewalks of Graceland Plaza and in the rooms of the Days Inn and other motels nearby, where pilgrims congregated. And while much of what was being offered in those days—Elvis clocks, lamps, and placemats—did not technically qualify under the heading of relics, since it had never been in direct or even indirect contact with Elvis, some of it did, including the "Original Elvis Wrist Watch" for sale in 1989 in room #282 of the Days Inn, with an opening bid of $700.

In those days, there were also ubiquitous trays of original Elvis amateur photographs for sale or trade that were and are valued much less as documents of specific events than as almost-tactile appropriations of Elvis, as his handprint or footprint might be. There is an obvious parallel here with the likes of the *Mandylion* of Edessa, the Shroud of Turin, and Juan Diego's *tilma* showing Our Lady of Guadalupe; in each case, a unique image of a charismatic figure is captured on an object, and through that capture, the object is transformed at once into a relic and a sacred image. Even the notion of touch is involved, at least as we look back toward Byzantium, since that was a time when seeing was understood to be touching. Saint Augustine, echoing the general belief of the period, imagined sight as both active and tactile as he described "that ray from our eye, with which we touch whatever we behold." For most Graceland tourists and pilgrims, the most valued souvenirs of their visit have always been their own photographs—of Graceland, of its multiple Elvis look-alikes, and of themselves and the group with which they came. These are unique appropriations of Graceland and, by extension, of Elvis, specific to a moment, and ardent fans sometimes use them on subsequent visits as central

FIG. 112

elements in their votives, which constitute an accretion of images over time—in some cases going all the way back to the living Elvis (fig. 112).

Whether because of the policing efforts of the Estate or simply because Internet trading is more convenient, or a combination of the two, Graceland in mid-August is no longer the venue it once was for securing Elvis stuff. What little trade in Elvis relics there is on site nowadays during Elvis Week is conducted out of a few dark rooms of the shabby little Scottish Inn & Suites a few hundred yards north of Graceland on Elvis Presley Boulevard. Its marquee announces the Fans of the King Collectible Show, though that consists of just five committed dealer rooms, only two or three of which are open at any given time. Generally, there is little difference in product line between the trinkets offered by the Scottish Inn & Suites dealers, including Frances Denney with her Elvis Presley Charms, and those available in the many nearly identical EPE-owned and -operated shops in Graceland Plaza and Graceland Crossing.

The exception is photography. Rockin' Robin Rosaaen, founder and president of All The King's Things, Inc., of San Jose, California, reputedly the biggest dealer in Elvis photographs with an inventory of more than 80,000 originals, shuffles quickly through the limited stock of Elvis snapshots being offered by Arnie Ganem of Moon

Over Miami, which are filed in shoe boxes on one of the two beds in room #110, just off the courtyard. While Arnie claims that highly unusual photographs of the King can trade in five figures, the price points for everyday Elvis photographic fare ("Elvis in leather jacket greeting fans at Music Gate, ca. 1970") are acknowledged and respected: $40 for an original and $3 for its copy (fig. 113).

It is the belief of the few who make the trip to Memphis in mid-August to deal in Elvis collectibles that the Estate wants nothing to do with them; or, more accurately, that the Estate wants to put them out of business at this location. Indeed, the one shop proximate to the mansion that does not belong to Elvis Presley Enterprises, Boulevard Souvenirs, not only stocks a refreshingly different line of Graceland T-shirts and EP trinkets—as well as the recently published *Elvis for Dummies,* which otherwise is nowhere to be found near Graceland—it announces defiantly with a banner draped across its façade that (2009): "We have 11 years left on our lease." That the Estate has chosen not to facilitate trade in or the authentication of such Elvis relics puts it in the company of the Vatican, whose controversy-averse corporate ethos keeps the likes of the Shroud of Turin at arm's length. For the folks who run the Presley home and all related commercial enterprises, it is all about business, and their business does not reside in the August Elvis Week crowd, whose pilgrim-like mentality accounts for a relatively small proportion of Graceland's traffic. After all, Graceland didn't get to be America's second most visited home, after the White House, because those tens of thousands of families who park their SUVs across from Graceland Mansion during their single, brief visit believe that a miraculous healing awaits them in the Meditation Garden.

An after-hours accident at Graceland in the early '90s provides a window onto the sanitized thinking

FIG. 113

of Graceland's management. It seems that Jerry Lee Lewis, who always thought of himself as the "true king," had just been released from the hospital after an operation to repair his alcohol-ravaged stomach. No rich foods and certainly no liquor were his doctor's departing instructions. So what did Jerry Lee do? He got drunk, ate a greasy chicken steak sandwich, and then, some time after midnight, did what he reputedly had done at least once before: he got into his Cadillac, raced north on Elvis Presley Boulevard, took a sudden sharp right, and smashed into Graceland's Music Gates. EPE was intent on fixing things before the tourists arrived the next morning and so they called on the blacksmiths from The National Ornamental Metal Museum—Memphis's contribution to a unique-to-Memphis genre of art museum. These skilled craftsmen, who otherwise spend their time building elaborate wrought-iron staircases for new *antebellum*-style mansions, arrived on site and went to work. The right wing of the gate was easily repaired but the left wing needed some serious work, back at the foundry, which took hours. In the process a number of pieces of the original gate had to be replaced. The foundry folks had what they thought was a brilliant idea: why not cut those discarded pieces into small sections, mount them on elegant little wooden blocks, label them as "authentic" pieces of the Music Gates, and then sell them to raise money for charity? This was something that Elvis would have done and that Graceland in the early postmortem years used to do. But the EPE powers that be, specifically, Executive Director Jack Soden, said no. The result was that those scraps of Graceland's Music Gates mostly stayed around the foundry of the museum, and with the telling of this story to a sympathetic listener, the top of the damaged pin upon which the left wing of the Music Gates had swung pre-Jerry Lee, ended up in the author's living room: "Hi Elvis. See you again in Heaven...."

Votives

The votive (*votum* or vow), the thing left behind, is the final piece to the Elvis/Graceland pilgrimage puzzle. As we have already seen, the Christian pilgrim not only took something away from the *locus sanctus* (a relic, a "blessing," a medallion), he usually left something behind. It might be an elaborate, custom-made image set up in a prominent place in the *martyrion* to acknowledge publicly the pilgrim's

FIG. 114

encounter with his spiritual friend, or it might be an anonymous personal item, like the "bracelets, rings, tiaras, plaited girdles, and belts" which according to the Piacenza pilgrim, were draped "in vast numbers" over the Tomb of Christ. Or it might be a simple greeting or prayer hastily drawn on any available surface, like that in the Chapel of Saint Vartan beneath the Church of the Holy Sepulchre, which shows a pilgrim's boat and bears the words "O Lord, we have come" (fig. 114). Each is a votive, and in its various forms a votive could serve at once as a record of the pilgrim's visit, as a perpetuation of his devotional contact with his "friend," and as a thank-you for a blessing received or anticipated.

Pilgrim votive inscriptions were common at early Byzantine pilgrim shrines. Many simply recorded the names of the pilgrims themselves or of friends or relatives who were unable to make the journey; the latter was the case for the Piacenza pilgrim at Cana, who wrote the names of his parents on the couch where Jesus had reclined:

> *Three miles further on...we came to Cana, where the Lord attended the wedding, and we actually reclined on the couch [where the Lord had reclined]. On it (undeserving though I am) I wrote the names of my parents....*

FIG. 115

Others acknowledged help received. A 7th-century source describes a votive scribbled in fiery red paint at the entrance to the healing shrine of Saints Cyrus and John near Alexandria, Egypt, by a certain "John," from Rome, who received his sight after waiting faithfully at the shrine for eight years. There is a dazzling variety of contemporary votives (*Milagros*) around the statue of Juan Diego at the Shrine of our Lady of Guadalupe, and we have already seen the crutches and thank-you plaques at the Oratory of Saint Joseph and the crutches and prosthetic limbs at Chimayo. Those votive testaments to the healings that are part of Chimayo year round are complemented during Holy Week—leading up to Good Friday, the anniversary of the shrine's original sanctifying event in 1813—by votive crosses of all sorts. Most are small and fabricated from available twigs or from fronds used by the faithful just a few days earlier, on Palm Sunday. Some, however, are very large and have been carried on the backs of penitent pilgrims, in imitation of Christ, from as far away as Albuquerque. This act of penance is itself the vehicle for the invocation of divine intervention on behalf of the sick (fig. 115):

> *May God through His*
> *loving kindness + mercy*
> *heal the body of my*
> *Beautiful Aunt…*

Votives are a central part of the life of Graceland year around, but in mid-August the variety and quantity of Elvis votives reaches a whole new level. There are three dominant media—candles, flowers, and magic markers—with those votives comprising flowers and/or candles often including images as well, mostly printed pictures of Elvis, though sometimes photographs of the fans themselves. Important sub-categories of Elvis votives include the off-the-shelf sort—mostly teddy bears and little angels—as well as the home-made prayer-poem messages and various iconographic tableaux that may be complemented by flowers. Flowers dominate the mix of votives at the grave proper and, in the form of arrangements on display stands, are found exclusively (except on the night of August 15) in the Meditation Garden and along the top portion of the path leading to it (fig. 116). The use of votive candles is generally confined to August 15, as they are part of the Candlelight Vigil and are integrated into the temporary votive shrines set up that evening on Elvis Presley Boulevard once it has been closed to traffic. These will invariably be coupled with pictures and statuary, and sometimes with flowers. Finally, the magic marker votives— which take the form of graffiti—are confined by the rules of Graceland to the Fans' Memorial Wall, where they are added daily (figs. 117, 118). This fieldstone barrier that sets off the grounds of Graceland proper from the sidewalk and Boulevard is about 175 yards long and six feet high, and at any given time has in excess of 10,000 fan messages, some of which, as we have seen, are accompanied by hurried sketches. The frontage road that conveniently branches off Elvis Presley Boulevard along the

FIG. 116

Wall allows fans in cars easily to pull off and write their message before they move on. For many years now, the Estate has taken care to employ someone to sand blast away messages, especially those with garish white backgrounds, to free up space for new messages and to keep an appropriate level of consistency (fig. 119).

The flowers at graveside and the nearby floral arrangements have been part of Graceland's votive mix from the beginning; it is said that United Florists, Inc. had its greatest sales ever in those few days just after Elvis died. Individual flowers to the left and right of the Elvis tomb slab are complemented by teddy bears of all sizes, some inscribed, and by angels, mostly in the form of winged children in sorrowful poses. Some flowers will be offered in containers that are themselves evocative of Elvis, such as a miniature pink Cadillac. Many of the floral arrangements

FIG. 117, FIG. 118, FIG. 119

on stands nearby are clearly made to order by local professionals, and typically convey a simple message such as the name of the responsible Elvis fan club and its country of origin, often indicated by a floral flag (fig. 120). Or the arrangement may simply take the form of a large "E" comprised of roses, perhaps with a golden crown on the top and Elvis's motto "TCB" affixed to the front, next to some musical notes. Some among these store-bought arrangements are crosses embellished with flowers and accompanied by a picture of Elvis (fig. 121). The home-made iconographic creations are more varied and creative. In 2009, a votive from "the Alabama girls" consisted of a heart broken into two sections, upper left and lower right, with a swath of Elvis postcard size pictures in between and a string of small white flowers around the edge. The right half of the heart bore the names of the five girls from Alabama—Joan, Connie, Debbie, Della, and Charlene—beneath the affirmation of "Love Always," while the left half bore this free-verse poem:

> *Our hearts leap when*
> *we behold*
> *Your pouty [sic] lips and*
> *musical soul.*

FIG. 120

FIG. 121

On August 16 your
Soul He did take
And left us all with
a HUGE heartbreak.

Nearby was a large multi-media votive whose iconography responded to the fact that 2009 marked the 40th anniversary of Elvis's return to Las Vegas in 1969 (fig. 122). It bore the words "What happens in Vegas / Started at Graceland," with Las Vegas evoked by a miniature stretch limousine and Graceland by a leafy white picket fence, and the two connected by a miniature version of the *Lisa Marie* airplane. We have already seen how some of these votives are designed to connect Elvis with the Mediation Garden and to inspire identification with and empathy from the fans gathered there, and others are designed to invoke compositionally Elvis's role as protector and comforter. Finally, there are those, like that from the Memphis Mafia fan club described in Chapter I, whose explicit intent is to "take care of Elvis's legacy."

The graffito messages on the Fans' Memorial Wall are Graceland's counterpart

FIG. 122

to the 4th-century pilgrim sketch in the Chapel of Saint Vartan. A small proportion are cynical and mean-spirited—"Next Time, Elvis, Just say NO"—but these will usually be covered over quickly by censoring fans. Most offer only a pilgrim's name, often with his or her hometown and the date. Affirmations of love for Elvis, almost exclusively from women—"I Love You Elvis, Debbie"—and often qualified by "eternal" or "forever," are common, as are votive inscriptions that incorporated titles or words from Elvis's songs: *Love Me Tender*, (*Let Me Be Your*) *Teddy Bear,* and *I'm so Lonesome I Could Cry*. Some fan messages, echoing the *vitae*, are angry and combative, and addressed to the "other"—"The King never did drugs"—but most are sweet and sentimental, and are addressed directly to Elvis. Beyond the hundreds of simple confessions of eternal love and devotion ("Elvis, I miss you and love you tender— Loving you, Annette"), there are scores of messages carrying raw, seemingly spontaneous evocations of sorrow or loss, like the one we have already seen, from Ralph:

> *8-16-77 is the saddest day of*
> *my life. I was too young to realize*
> *it at the time. I was ten.*
>
> *Love*
>
> *Ralph*

And there are many references to an eventual rendezvous of the devotee with Elvis: "Will wait for you and see you later in Paradise. Erika" and "See U in Heaven. Ellen." Others, in much the same tone, offer thanks for Elvis's spiritual intervention, as in "Thank you Elvis for always being there when I needed you the most." In "Carla's" votive, the writer and reader both understand these words as evoking an on-going relationship with the postmortem Elvis:

> *Elvis*
>
> *Thanks*
>
> *for all you helped me through.*
> *I wouldn't be me*
> *without you.*
> *See you in heaven.*
> *I love you*
> *Carla.*

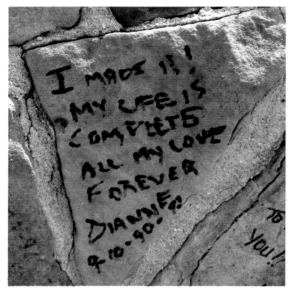

FIG. 123

Other inscriptions reference the very act of pilgrimage within the framework of the notion of liminality by asserting that this act and this moment offer a profound sense of fulfillment (Fig. 123):

> *I MADE IT!*
> *MY LIFE IS*
> *COMPLETE*
> *ALL MY LOVE*
> *FOREVER*
> *DIANNE*

There are inscriptions that speak directly to the continuity of Elvis veneration from generation to generation: "3rd Generation ELVIS LOVER. Thank you." And even those that suggest how that continuity was achieved: "We teach our young about you. Marie."

Christianity asserts itself in many ways on the Fans' Memorial Wall, sometimes almost playfully, as in "Give us this day our daily Elvis. Sam." But more often, religion appears through the simple substitution of "Elvis" where one would otherwise understand and expect "God" or "Jesus," as in "ELVIS Lives in our Hearts" and "Elvis is Love." A rare inscriptional elegance is achieved when that substitution of Elvis for the Christian divinity can be framed within the words of one of his songs (fig. 124):

> *HOW GREAT*
> *THOU ART ELVIS*
> *COLETTE*

Some votives almost suggest an intercessory role for Elvis. First, we learn the expected, namely, that: "Jesus Loves Elvis." But not so far away, we discover that: "JESUS LOVES THOSE THAT LOVE ELVIS." There is "Elvis Lives" coupled with a radiating Calvary Cross (fig. 125), and the assertion that Elvis's work in life, and perhaps still, is to "take care of business" on Christ's behalf:

FIG. 123

[Calvary Cross]

TCB

4

Christ

Amy Smith

Perhaps it is not such a great leap to the next level, where "God is Elvis" and "ELVIS IS LORD" (fig. 126), with the latter qualified in a second had by the word "IDOLATRY." And the logical implication of that linkage is captured in the votive, which is to be read sequentially, this time with two editorial overlays (fig. 1):

ELVIS   JESUS   ELVIS
DIED   DIED   DIED
FOR   FOR   FOR
OUR   OUR   HIS
SINS   SINS   SINS
YOU FOOL

For some, at least, it would seem that Elvis and Jesus are one, and their work is the same: salvation for their followers.

How should this last three-part inscription be understood? Statistically, we can be pretty sure that all three voices are believers; 92% of Americans believe in God or some higher power, and the Graceland subset is certainly even more devout. Writer #1 frames his or her votive in traditional Christian terms, simply

FIG. 125
FIG. 126

substituting Elvis for Jesus, much like the Crown-of-Thorns Elvis tattoo. We may assume, but we cannot be certain, that the Graceland votive writer, the tattooist, and the tattooed were all sincere. Writer #3, on the other hand, should probably be assigned to the same camp of cynics as the author of: "Next Time, Elvis, Just say NO." But what of the middle writer, who calls the first writer a fool and corrects him or her by writing Jesus over Elvis? Perhaps this person's sensibility would align with that of Linda Thompson, Elvis's former girlfriend, who in her Elvis Week 2009 interview over Sirius Radio made it absolutely clear that Graceland was not a place for miracles just as she recalled, with some wonder, how her LA apartment, alone in its complex, lost electricity the day Elvis died. Writer #1 is certainly at level three on the celebrity-worship scale, and that may even be true of writer #2, though cynical writer #3 is likely just a tourist or, at most, a level one casual fan.

But maybe there is a more subtle reading of this three-phase exchange. Perhaps writer #1 was not thinking of mankind's salvation (as otherwise realized through Jesus's Crucifixion) but rather of "our sins" as they relate specifically to Elvis the "martyr." He or she would be fully aware of the generally-held conviction among Elvis fans that *they* killed him by demanding too much of him and by not taking proper care of him. Writer #2, by this reasoning, would simply have misunderstood the true intent and meaning of the original writer. Writer #3, on the other hand, might be fan of the second level of intensity (i.e., a EP fan club member), who was simply clear-headed enough to have long since concluded the obvious, namely, that while Elvis was a pretty special person, he made some very big mistakes along the way that eventually killed him.

IV.
LOOKING AHEAD

Jerusalem has been a major pilgrimage destination for 17 centuries. At times, because of the city's turbulent history as a holy place for three of the world's great religions, pilgrim traffic has slowed to a trickle, but it has always come back—as has pilgrimage to the Cathedral of Santiago de Compostela, in Spain, with its relics of Saint James, especially in the last generation, when *El Camino,* the Way of Saint James, has become "the thing to do." The Shrine of Our Lady of Guadalupe continues to attract millions of pilgrims annually, nearly five centuries after the Lady of Heaven miraculously imprinted Juan Diego's *tilma* with her image, as does the Shrine of Our Lady of Lourdes, 150 years after the Immaculate Conception appeared to young Bernadette at the Sacred Grotto. The tiny *Sanctuario de Chimayo* is still thriving 200 years after a local shepherd encountered a radiating crucifix in a hole in the ground. Traffic to Mecca during the *Hajji* has increased nearly 50% in the last decade, to nearly 3 million pilgrims.

By contrast, Simeon's shrine has been abandoned for centuries and the Shrine of Brother André in Montreal, despite its imposing architecture, is relatively quiet nowadays; its wooden votive crutches, contrasting with their aluminum counterparts at Chimayo, tell their own story. Pilgrimage to see the "Holy Shroud" in the Gothic cloister of Cadouin Abbey in south-central France was fashionable a century ago, but came to a virtual halt when its sacred cloth was eventually discredited by textile historians. By contrast, the Shroud of Turin's great fame as a pilgrimage destination is a phenomenon of just the last century, thanks to an amateur photographer named Secondo Pia, who in 1898 was astonished to discover that his glass-plate negative of the Shroud "miraculously" generated a powerful, sculptural image of Christ from the faint sepia tones of the Shroud itself.

The fall of the Iron Curtain brought with it an enormous increase in traffic to Auschwitz-Birkenau and visitation is likely to grow further as access from nearby

FIG. 127

Krakow is upgraded. Similarly, pilgrimage to Ground Zero is certain to be among New York City's major attractions once the National September 11 Memorial and Museum is completed. The Grassy Knoll in Dallas and the Lorraine Motel in Memphis are likely to continue to welcome their small, steady stream of visitors, so long as their respective charismatic martyrs retain their attraction for political and social idealists and the conspiracy theories for both deaths continue to be debated; moreover, the magnetism of both is enhanced by their relic-filled local museums. Jim Morrison's grave in Père-Lachaise Cemetery will also likely continue to be an attraction, as it has been for the last 40 years, thanks to the inherent liminality of his marijuana and alcohol culture, *The Doors*' still-popular music, and the drama of his premature death.

Indeed, there was a large and mostly somber crowd gathered at Jim's grave-side on July 3, 2011, to mark the 40th anniversary of his passing (fig. 127). Most of the assembled fans were under the age of 40, a number were clearly drunk, and there was a lingering scent of marijuana in the morning air. Coincidently, Princess Di's 50th birthday fell on July 1, just two days before the anniversary of Morrison's death. In contrast with the bustling scene in Section 6 of Père-Lachaise, the scene around the *Flamme de la Liberté* in the Place de l'Alma, which had been co-opted for and covered with Diana and Dodi votives just hours after their death and for years thereafter (fig. 128), was by July 2011 quiet and dispassionate; moreover, fatal pillar #13 was all but ignored. Perhaps the royal wedding of Diana's son Edward, seen by 3 billion people world-wide, will begin to reverse that trend, and in any event, it sets up the possibility if not the inevitability of some form of dynastic succession for her/his/their cult. And as for Michael Jackson, it is not yet clear whether the Gloved One, postmortem, is on the ascent or the decline, though the absence of an acknowledged paramount Jackson *locus sanctus*, with body and relics, will inevitably militate against his ever reaching the Elvis/Graceland level.

FIG. 128

The Elvis/Graceland phenomenon was chosen as the subject of this book because it is a Category 5 within its genre of secular charismatic martyrs with *loca sancta*: more people, more intensely. The Introduction to this book laid out an image of Graceland during Elvis Week in 2009 that differed little in scale and intensity from the Graceland of mid-August 20 years earlier. Yet many in the cast of '89—which already included its own "new generation"—had been replaced by '09. How did that happen, and will it continue? Is the answer totally guesswork or is it susceptible to critical thinking? In attempting to answer these questions, it is useful to reconsider the nature of "conversion" to Elvis devotion as we have encountered it in this book. According to votives on the Fans' Memorial Wall, Elvis is taught by grown-ups ("Marie") to the young, there is a third-generation "Elvis Lover" who self-identifies ("Megan" from Seattle), and there are attested moments of conversion ("8-13-95"), after which intense pilgrimage behavior kicks in ("June" from Oklahoma). On site, in 2009, there was the wheel-chair

FIG. 129

bound "David" from Arkansas, who identified himself as a third-generation devotee who was converted on-site at Graceland at age 18 and was in the process of passing his Elvis devotion down yet another generation, to his three-year-old nephew. And there was the ubiquitous 9-year-old tribute artist named "Trenten" with his facilitating stage father at his side (fig. 129).

At the heart of this "perpetuation potential" for Graceland, or any other secular *locus sanctus,* are the complementary ideas of liminality and *communitas.* The former constitutes the aggregate of forces that facilitate conversion and the latter revolves around the clarity of the boundary that differentiates the converted from others. Consider Steve Prefontaine, sometimes called the "James Dean of Track" because, like Dean, he was a rebel and died young in a car accident. Despite the facts that Prefontaine's body is interred at Sunset Memorial Park in his hometown of Coos Bay, Oregon, his running relics are on display in the Oregon Sports Hall of Fame in Portland, and his death *locus,* Pre's Rock, is just east of the University of Oregon in Eugene, his small circle of running devotees has been replicated over nearly two generations. Why? In part, because there is a powerful sense of *communitas* among long distance runners, who continue to be inspired by Pre's challenge "To give anything less than your best is to sacrifice the gift," and in part, perhaps, because the runner's high (with its endocannabinoids) is inherently liminal.

Liminality in the world of Elvis and Graceland is facilitated everywhere by the continuing popularity and power of Elvis music and by the thousands of Elvis tribute artists who bring that music to life around the world. At Graceland, where Elvis' lifestyle has been frozen in time, there is the persuasive force of Elvis relics year round and, of course, the very body of Elvis. And these are complemented, within a day's drive, by the Elvis birth house, the Elvis high school, and the Elvis recording studio, among other ancillary Elvis *loca santa*. During Elvis Week there is the compounding power toward liminality of sacred time (including the heat), as well as the ever-present Elvis look-alikes and tribute artists, who are especially adept at tapping into Elvis's charisma and electrifying the liminality of the moment for those first-timers made susceptible by the power of the surroundings (recall the oxygen inside the front door of the Mansion). There is the affecting private ritual of the early morning Walk Up and the awe-inspiring public ritual of the Candlelight Vigil, with its accompanying homily, Elvis hymns, and Walk Up. And finally, there is the intense cohesion and sense of differentiation that exists among the *communitas* of Elvis converts ("he was one of us"), who tend to share geographic, economic, educational, religious, and ethnic characteristics in common, and together nurture an abhorrence for the "other," which includes the media, the Estate, Michael Jackson fans, and those who "just don't get it." Elvis Presley, Graceland, Elvis Week, and Presley pilgrims have all been created out of and continue to be nourished by an all-but-unique convergence of complementary forces toward liminality and *communitas*—which suggests that we should not be looking for significant change any time soon.

A final question: is the Elvis/Graceland phenomenon now or might it ever become a "religion"? Much has been written about this question in the tabloids, and even in academic journals, and yes, there are—or at least have been—a variety of Elvis "churches," including the 24-Hour (storefront) Church of Elvis in Portland, Oregon. But what do these mostly high-camp and ephemeral manifestations of

Elvis "churchness" have to do with religion? After all, there is no Elvis theology, no Elvis hierarchy of clergy, no characteristic Elvis sanctuary design, and no Elvis intercession, nor are there Elvis sacraments or Elvis congregations—certainly not in the sense that all of these are understood within the context of the world's great religions.

What is flawed in attempts to interpret the Elvis/Graceland phenomenon within the framework of conventional religion are not the (mostly murky) answers, but rather the question itself. The religious dimension of the Elvis/Graceland phenomenon should not be sought in its relative alignment with the central theological and organizational building blocks of the world's great religions; rather, it should be sought on religion's "edges"—in the much less organized and structured world of charismatics, holy places, and pilgrimage that all religions, to some degree, share in common. Elvis, like Saint Simeon 15 centuries before him, and Juan Diego, Bernadette Soubirous, and Brother André along the way, and Graceland, like Qal`at Sem`an and Chimayo, find their home not at the center but rather on the boundaries of conventional religion, where they are enthusiastically supported by the many,

FIG. 130

viewed with skepticism by the elite few, and remain substantially free of hierarchical control. If we turn from the notion that the postmortem Elvis might someday, somehow engender a religion analogous to Christianity or Buddhism, or even a sect within Christianity, to the idea that the Elvis/Graceland phenomenon is already comfortably situated within a familiar para-religious world, then the elegant clarity and simplicity emerges, and Elvis and all the martyred charismatics like him are understood for what they are: the saints of our day.

ILLUSTRATIONS

Unless otherwise indicated, the photographs are by the author; Graceland photographs without dates were taken in 2009.

BIBLIOGRAPHY

ABC NEWS Nightline, "Remembering Elvis," August 14, 1987, Show #1624

Simon Akam, "A Makeshift World Trade Center Shrine Returns to Ground Zero," *The New York Times*, August 25, 2009

Sabine Albersmeier *et al.*, *Heroes: Mortals and Myths in Ancient Greece* (Baltimore, 2009)

Tim Arango, "Hold the Phone! That Sure Sounds Like Saddam Hussein," *The New York Times*, April 11, 2011

Gêrard Ausina and Luigi Prodomi, *Lourdes: The Life of Bernadette, the Apparitions, the Shrines* (Lourdes, n.d.)

Martina Bagnoli *et al.*, *Treasures of Heaven: Saints, Relics, and Devotion in Medieval Europe* (Baltimore, 2010)

Dan Barry, "What We kept," *The New York Times,* September 11, 2011

Bill Beeny, *Final proof: The King IS Alive!* (n.p., n.d.)

Gail Brewer-Giorgio, *Is Elvis Alive?* (???, 1988)

M. Broshi and Gabriel Barkay, "Excavations in the Chapel of St. Vartan in the Holy Sepulchre," *Israel Exploration Journal*, 35 (1985), 125ff.

Peter Brown, *The Cult of the Saints: Its Rise and Function in Latin Christianity* (Chicago, 1982)

L. S. Bunting and B. Stelter, "Dancing in the Streets to Remember Michael Jackson," *The New York Times*, Art Beat, June 26, 2009

Julie Bykowicz, "World Trade Center beams arrive for 9/11 memorial," *The Baltimore Sun*, November 24, 2010

R. A. Chestnut, *Devoted to Death:* Santa Muerte, *the Skeleton Saint* (Oxford, 2012)

Pamela Colloff, "Dreaming of Her," *Texas Monthly* (April, 2010), 86ff.

Alan Cowell, "A horror that is best not forgotten," *International Herald Tribune*, June 25-26, 2011

Brigitte and Gilles Delluc, *Vister l'abbaye de Cadouin* (Luçon, FR, 1992), 23ff.

Judy Dempsey, "Hitler Aide's Grave Is Removed To Stop Neo-Nazi Pilgrimages," *The New York Times,* July, 21, 2011

Verena Dobnik, "Museum goes inside Ground Zero," *The New York Times*, ???

Susan Doll, *Elvis for Dummies* (Hoboken, NJ, 2009)

Rachael Donadio, "A Pope's Beatification Stirs Excitement and Dissension," *The New York Times*, April 29, 2011

Robert Doran, intro. and trans., *The Lives of Simeon Stylites*, Cistercian Studies, 112 (Kalamazoo, MI, 1992)

Erika Doss, *Elvis Culture: Fans, Faith, and Image* (Lawrence, KA, 1999)

Michael Dresser and Tricia Bishop, "Friends Mark Charles Village Victim's Birthday at Makeshift Memorial," *The Baltimore Sun*, July 27, 2010

11th Annual Candlelight Service, August 15, 1989 (program)

Elvis Fever Fan Club Quarterly, Baltimore, 1988

"Elvis is Alive!" *Weekly World News*, May 24, 1988

"Elvis, the Untold Story," *National Enquirer*, September 6, 1977

Sidney Ember, "Art From The Heart," *The New York Times,* September 11, 2011

Eusebius, Life of Constantine, Av. Cameron and S. G. Hall, trans. (Oxford, 1999)

David Farley, *An Irreverent Curiosity: In Search of the Church's Strangest Relic in Italy's Oddest Town* (Los Angeles, 2009)

Faith and Transformation: Votive Offerings and Amulets from the Alexander Girard Collection, D. Francis, ed. (Santa Fe, 2007)

Karen V. Fernandez and John L. Lastovicka, "Making Magic: Fetishes in Contemporary Consumption," *Journal of Consumer Research*, 38 (2011), ???

Roy J. Ferrari, trans., *Saint Basil: The Letters,* Loeb Classical Library, I-IV (Cambridge, MA, London, 1950-1953)

John Frow, "Is Elvis a God? Cult, Culture, Questions of Method," *International Journal of Cultural Studies* 1, no. 2 (1998), 197-210

Judy Fruchter Minkove, "The boy downstairs," *The Baltimore Sun*, January 8, 2004

Paul D. Garrett, "Canonization," *Sacred Art Journal*, 11/2 (1990), 55ff.

G. Garvey, "Fan Pays a King's Ransom for Elvis Shirts at Auction," *Chicago Tribune*, October, 19, 2009

Malcolm Gay, "Giving Up the Memorabilia, But Not the Belief: Elvis Lives," *The New York Times*, November 8, 2007

Larry Geller and Joel Spector, with Patricia Romanowski, *If I Can Dream: Elvis' Own Story* (New York, 1989)

S. Goldberg, J. Margolin, and J. Fermino, "Forever Etched In," *New York Post*, September 12, 2011

Albert H. Goldman, *Elvis* (New York, *et al.,* 1981)

Adriana Gomez Licon and Felipe Larios, "Mexican border family suspected of human sacrifice," Associate Press, April 1, 2012

Irina Gorainoff, *Les fols en Christ dans la tradition orthodoxe* (Brouwer, ???, 1983)

André Grabar, *Early Christian Art: AD 200-395: From the Rise of Christianity to the Death of Theodosius* (New York, 1968)

L. Grove, "Saint Elvis," *The Washington Post*, August 12, 1987

Alma Guillermoprieto, "Mexican Saints," *National Geographic* (May, 2010)

Peter Guralnick, *Last Train to Memphis: The Rise of Elvis Presley* (Boston *et al.*, 1994)

Peter Guralnick, *Careless Love: The Unmaking of Elvis Presley* (Boston *et. al.,* 1999)

Boniface Hanley, *Brother Andre: All he could do was pray* (Montreal, 1979)

Lyndon Harris, "Sanctuary at Ground Zero," *National Geographic Magazine,* September, 2002

R. L. Harris, "Jackson Collectors Open Their Wallets at Auction," *The New York Times,* June 27, 2010

Anemona Hartocollis, "For 9/11 Museum, a Dispute Over Unidentified Remains," *The New York Times*, April 3, 2011

David M. Herszenhorn, "Mexicans Unite to Honor Their Spiritual Mother," *The New York Times,* December 13, 1998

Arthur Hirsch, "Saintly miracle?" *The Baltimore Sun,* June 28, 2009

Kenneth G. Holum and Gary Vikan, "The Trier Ivory, *Adventus* Ceremonial, and the Relics of St. Stephen," *Dumbarton Oaks Papers*, 33 (1979), 113ff.

B. J. Honsick, "Saints of America: A New Blossom of American Sanctity, New Martyr Priest John of Santa Cruz," *Orthodox World*, 21/3 (1985), 113

Jerry Hopkins and Danny Sugarman, *No One Here Gets Out Alive* (Medford, NJ, 1980)

Jamie Smith Hopkins, "Md. dedicates memorial to 9/11," *The Baltimore Sun*, September 12, 2011

Matthew Hutson, *The 7 Laws of Magical Thinking: How Irrational Beliefs Keep Us Happy, Healthy, and Sane* (New York, NY *et. Al*)

Erinn Hutkin, "Mini Graceland lives," *The Roanoke Times*, August 16, 2006

Icons of American Protestantism: The Art of Warner Sallman, David Morgan, ed. (New Haven, 1996)

John of Damascus, *Orthodox Faith*, F. H. Chase, trans., *The Fathers of the Church*, 37 (Washington, DC, 1958)

Elizabeth Kay, *Chimayo Valley Traditions* (Santa Fe, 1987)

John Kifner, "Amid Frenzy, Iranians Bury The Ayatollah," *The New York Times*, June 6, 1989

C. King, "His Truth Goes Marching On: Elvis Presley and the Pilgrimage to Graceland," *Pilgrimage in Popular Culture*, Ian Reader and Tony Walter, eds. (Houndsmills, Basingstoke, UK, 1993), 92ff.

Ernst Kitzinger, "The Cult of Images in the Age Before Iconoclasm," *Dumbarton Oaks Papers*, 8 (1954), 83ff.

Bernard Kötting, *Peregrinatio religiousa* (Regensberg, 1950)

Richard Krautheimer, "Introduction to an 'Iconography of Architecture'," *Journal of the Warburg and Courtauld Institutes,* 5 (1942), 1ff.

Gary Laderman, *Sacred Matters: Celebrity Worship, Sexual Ecstasies, the Living Dead, and Other Signs of Religious Life in the United States* (New York, NY, 2009)

G. Lichtman, "Saint Elvis: From Graceland to Jerusalem...," *The Jerusalem Post*, May 10, 1996

Ted Loos, "Architect and 9/11 Memorial Both Evolved Over the Years," *The New York Times,* September 4, 2011

Lourdes, J. Hausner, Director (2009)

Sarah Lyall, "A Traditional Royal Wedding, But for the 3 Billion Witnesses," *The New York Times,* April 30, 2011

Robert D. McFadden, "Pope John Paul II, Church Shepherd and a Catalyst for World Change," **The New York Times**, April 3, 2005

Marcii Magliulo, **Crosses Across Our Nation** (Penngrove, CA, 2005)

Henry Maguire, "Truth and Convention in Byzantine Descriptions of Works of Art," *Dumbarton Oaks Papers*, 28 (1974), 113ff.

"'Makin' like Elvis' is curing my arthritis!," *Weekly World New*, October, 2, 1990

John Malty *et al.,* "Personality and Coping: A Context for Examining Celebrity Worship and Mental Health," **The British Journal of Psychology** 95 (2004), 411-428

Cyril Mango, "The Pilgrim's Motivation," **Akten des XII. Internationalen Kongresses für Christliche Archäologie (Bonn, 22-28 September 1991). JAC, Ergänzungsband**, 20/1 (Münster, 1995), 1ff.

May Mann, *Elvis: Why Don't they Leave you Alone* (New York, 1982)

Pierre Maraval, *Lieux saints et pelerinages d'orient* (Paris, 2004)

Karal Ann Marling, *Graceland: Going Home with Elvis* (Cambridge, MA, 1996)

Lynn E. McCutcheon *et al.,* "Conceptualization and Measurement of Celebrity Worship," *The British Journal of Psychology* 93 (2002), 69-81?

C. Austin Miles, "In the Garden," 1912

Mondo Elvis: The Strange Rites & Rituals of the King's Most Devoted Disciples, Tom Corby, director (Rhino Video, 1984)

Raymond A. Moody, Jr., *Elvis After Life: Unusual Psychic Experiences Surrounding the Death of a Superstar* (New York, *et al.*, 1987)

Neil K. Moran, *Singers in Late Byzantine and Slavonic Painting*, Byzantina Neerlandica, 9 (Leiden, 1986)

Kim Murphy, "Mexican Robin Hood Gains a Kind of Notoriety in U.S.," *The New York Times,* February 8, 2008

Seth Mydans, "From Village Boy to Soldier, Martyr and, Many Say, 'Saint'," *The New York Times*, November 21, 2003

George E. Newman, Gil Diesendruck, and Paul Bloom, "Celebrity Contagion and the Value of Objects," *Journal of Consumer Research,* 38 (2011), ???

Mary Lee and Sidney Nolan, *Christian Pilgrimage in Modern Western Europe* (Chapel Hill, NC, 1989)

Robert Ousterhout, "*Loca Sancta* and the Architectural Responses to Pilgrimage," R. Ousterhout, ed., *The Blessings of Pilgrimage, Illinois Byzantine Studies,* I (Urbana, Chicago, 1990), 108ff.

"Painting of Elvis weeps real tears," *Weekly World News*, November 1, 1988

Parade Magazine, August 9, 1987

Evelyne Patlagean, "Ancient Byzantine hagiography and social history," *Saints and their Cults: Studies in Religious Sociology, Folklore and History* (Cambridge, UK, *et al.*, 1985), ???

David W. Phillipson, *Ancient Churches of Ethiopia* (New Haven, 2009)

"Photo of Elvis Cured my Cancer," *Weekly World News*, December 29, 1987

Russell A. Potter, "Tupac's Posthumous Live Tour," *The New York Times*, April 20, 2012

Patricia Jobe Pierce, *The Ultimate Elvis* (New York, NY, 1994)

Ian Reader, "Conclusions," *Pilgrimage in Popular Culture*, Ian Reader and Tony Walter, eds. (Houndsmills, Basingstoke, UK, 1993), 220ff.

Gretchen Reynolds, "Like It or Not, our Brains Are Enticing Us to Run," *The New York Times,* May 1, 2012

James Riordan and Jerry Prochnicky, *Break on Through: The Life and Death of Jim Morrison* (???, 1991)

G. Roberts, "They called him The Man Who Killed Elvis: Now the star's doctor finally reveals the true madness of the King's final days," *Daily Mail*, January 14, 2010

G. Roberts and H. Fountain, "A Place for the Past and Future," *The New York Times,* September 11, 2011

Larry Rohter, "In a Most Unsaintly City, a Bandit Wears a Halo," *The New York Times,* May 11, 1989

Larry Rohter, "A Legend Grows, and So Does an Industry," *The New York Times*, January 12, 1997

Ron Rosenbaum, "ELVIS HEALER," *The New York Times Magazine,* September 24, 1995

Edward Rothstein, "Remembering Lower Manhattan's Day of Horror, Without Pomp or Circumstance," *The New York Times*, September 11, 2007

Edward Rothstein, "Amid the Memorials, Ambiguity and Ambivalence," *The New York Times,* September 3, 2011

"Saint Elvis?" *Globe*, January 9, 1990

Sainthood: Its Manifestations in World Religions, R. Kieckhefer and G. D. Bond, eds. (Berkeley, 1988)

Saints and Their Cults: Studies in Religious Sociology, Folklore, and History, Stephen Wilson, ed., (New York, 1983)

Elaine Sciolino and Daniel J. Wakin, "Before Viewing, Procession for Pope Draws Thousands," *The New York Times*, April 5, 2005

Katharine Seelye, "A Sense of Closure at 9/11 Crash Site," *The New York Times,* September 10, 2011

David Segal, "Fame May Never Be the Same," *The New York Times*, June 27, 2009

R. W. Sellars and T. Walter, "From Custer to Kent State: Heroes, Martyrs and the Evolution of Popular Shrines in the USA," *Pilgrimage in Popular Culture,* Ian Reader and Tony Walter, eds. (Houndsmills, Basingstoke, UK, 1993), 179ff.

N. A. Silberman, "Elvis: The Myth Lives On," *Archaeology,* 43:4 (1990), 80

Jean-Pierre Sodini, "La hiérarchisation des espaces à Qal`at Sem`an," *Le Sacré et son incription dans l'espace à Byzance et en Occident: Études comparés*, M. Kaplan, ed., Byzantina Sorbonensia, 18 (Paris, 2001), 251ff.

Roberta Smith, "Three Ways To Look Back, None Easy," *The New York Times,* September 10, 2011

Ronald Smothers, "Scholars—on Elvis—Gathering at Ole Miss," *The New York Times,* August 5, 1995

John Snyder, *Northern Renaissance Art* (New York, 1985)

Jane Stern and Michael Stern, *Elvis World* (New York, Toronto, 1987)

Stanley J. Tambiah, *Magic, Science, Religion, and the Scope of Rationality* (Cambridge, MA, 1990)

George Tchalenko, *Villages antiques de la Syrie du Nord,* I, II (Paris, 1953)

The Elvis Reader: Texts and Sources on the King of Rock'n'Roll, Kevin Quain, ed. (New York, NY, 1992)

"The King gave me a caddy!" *Weekly World News*, July 23, 1991

"The King has Lived Many Times Before," *National Examiner*, March 6, 1990

The Life of Saint John Maximovich, Archbishop of Shanghai and San Francisco, DVD, G. Redmond and Aaron Freese, n.d.

The Nicene and Post Nicene Fathers, 2nd series, 11 (Grand Rapids, MI, 1955)

The Works of Saint Augustine, 3, Sermons, vol. 9, E. Hill, OP, trans. (Hyde Park, N.Y. and New York, 1994)

This is Elvis, Biopic/Documentary, A. Solt and M. Leo, Directors (1981)

C. C. Thompson II and J. P. Cole, *The Death of Elvis: What Really Happened* (New York, 1991)

William Thompson, "Words on the wall leave heartfelt passions to Elvis," *Baltimore Evening Sun*, August 13, 1987

A. Trolf, "Graceland Too: Paul MacLoed," Fecal Face Dot Com, Guest Blog (July 27, 2007)

Susan Tucker, "Pentecostalism and Popular Culture in the South: A Study of Four Musicians," *Journal of Popular Culture*, 16 (1982), 68ff.

Victor Turner and Edith Turner, *Image and Pilgrimage in Christian Culture: Anthropological Perspectives* (New York, 1978)

Kristi Turnquist, "It's Curtains for the Velveteria Velvet Painting Museum," *The Oregonian,* January 4, 2010

Ian Urbina, "As Roadside Memorials Multiply, a Second Look," *The New York Times*, February 6, 2006

Van Dam, *Glory of the Martyrs*, Translated Texts for Historians, Latin Series, III (Liverpool, 1988)

Paul van den Ven, *La vie ancienne de S. Syméon Stylite le Jeune (521-592)*, SubsHag, 32 (Brussels, 1962[I], 1970[II])

Gary Vikan, "Sacred Image, Sacred Power," *Icon: Four Essays*, G. Vikan, ed. (Washington, DC, 1988)

Gary Vikan, "Graceland as *Locus Sanctus*," *Elvis + Marilyn: 2x Immortal*, G. Pagnoli, ed. (New York, 1994), 150ff.

Gary Vikan, "Debunking the Shroud: Made by Human Hands," *Biblical Archaeology Review*, 24/6 (1998), 27ff.

Gary Vikan, *Early Byzantine Pilgrimage Art* (Washington, DC, 2010)

Peter W. L. Walker, *Holy City, Holy Places: Christian Attitudes to Jerusalem and the Holy Land in the Fourth Century* (Oxford, 1990)

Pete Ward, *Gods Behaving Badly: Media, Religion, and Celebrity Culture* (Waco, TX, 2011)

David Waters, "Elvis at 75: Long Live the king," *The Washington Post*, January 8, 2010

Max Weber, *Economy and Society*, I-III (New York, 1968 [1922])

"'Weeping Virgin' Icon Draws Throngs to Chicago," *The New York Times*, December 22, 1986

Kurt Weitzmann, *et al., The Icon* (New York, 1987)

Kurt Weitzmann, *The Monastery of Saint Catherine at Mount Sinai: The Icons, I, From the Sixth to the Tenth Century* (Princeton, 1976)

John Wilkinson, "The Tomb of Christ: An Outline of Its Structural History," *Levant*, 4 (1972), 83ff.

John Wilkinson, *Egeria's Travels*, 3rd ed. (Jerusalem and Warminster, UK, 1999)

John Wilkinson, intro. and trans., *Jerusalem Pilgrims Before the Crusades*, rev. ed. (Warminster, UK, 2002), *Travels from Piacenza,* 79ff.

Ian Wilson, *The Shroud: Fresh Light on the 2000-Year-Old Mystery...* (New York, NY, *et al.*, 2010)

Michael Wilson, "Trade Center Steel Forms Heart of Memorials," *New York Times*, September 7, 2009

Zachary Woolfe, "A Gift from the Musical Gods," *New York Times*, August 21, 2011

Semir Zeki, *Inner Vision: An Exploration of Art and the Brain* (Oxford, UK, 1999)

INDEX